Dorothea Ruggles-Brise

The musical miscellany:

A select collection of Scots, English and Irish songs, set to music

Dorothea Ruggles-Brise

The musical miscellany:
A select collection of Scots, English and Irish songs, set to music

ISBN/EAN: 9783337728656

Printed in Europe, USA, Canada, Australia, Japan

Cover: Foto ©ninafisch / pixelio.de

More available books at **www.hansebooks.com**

SELECT COLLECTION

———— of the ————

most approved

Scots, English, & Irish

SONGS,

set to Music.

PERTH:
Printed by J. Brown.
MDCCLXXXVI.

THE
MUSICAL MISCELLANY:

A

SELECT COLLECTION

OF

SCOTS, ENGLISH AND IRISH

SONGS,

SET TO

MUSIC.

PERTH:
PRINTED BY J. BROWN.
MDCCLXXXVI.

THE

PREFACE.

THE Editors of the following Compilation, unwilling to amufe the Public with an empty harangue, or a gaudy apparatus of words, by way of introduction to their Book; only beg leave to make the following obfervations :———

Since time immemorial, it has been allowed, that Mufic has always been efteemed an ancient and powerful Science.

We are informed, from Heathen Mythology, that Mufic was invented by Apollo, who was ftyled the God of Wifdom.

———*Per me concordant carmina nervis.*

OVIDI METAM.

THE PREFACE.

How mufic was cultivated in thofe early ages, impartial hiftory alone can tell. Suffice it to fay, that this elevating Science had it's patrons, and proficients, in moft ages and nations. And it is with pleafure we obferve, that this celeftial progeny has ftill it's abettors in our own country. The public attention paid by many Gentlemen of Scotland, to this polite and very neceffary part of education, is at once patriotic and laudable.

The Publifhers of the following sheets, look forward to that Golden Æra, when, they truft, that *Mufic* fhall not only attract the attention of fuperior minds, but when *it* fhall acquire that univerfal eftimation, that a *Science* fo fublime, richly deferves.

With a fincere view to promote this end, the following Collection of Songs, fet to Mufic, is, with all fubmiffion, offered to the *Public*. The Selectors of this Work, humbly ima-

THE PREFACE.

gine, they may without the leaſt ſhadow of vanity, aver, that *it* is the firſt Publication of the kind, ever attempted in *Scotland*.—The arrangement of the Words, as well as the Muſic, has been ſtudied with the greateſt attention; and being deſigned for the entertainment both of *Ladies* and *Gentlemen*, the ſtricteſt care has been taken, to avoid *indelicacy*.

Beſides a great number of modern Songs of real humour and taſte, there are alſo inſerted, a great variety of the moſt beautiful Scots Airs, to many of which, the Baſſes are added.

How far the Editors of this Work, have been ſuccefsful in the Selection they have made, Time and a candid Public, only muſt determine.

Let it only be obſerved in one word, that the *influence* of *Muſic* over the *human mind*, is fully evinced, by the Prince of Latin poetry.—Virgil, in his inimitable Eclogue, called *Silenus*, where, introducing Chromis and Mnasylus, two youthful swains, finding Silenus asleep in his cave, (often the Sire had amused them, with the promise of a song) and, in order to make him perform his engagement, they bind him with his own wreaths. He awaking, and smiling at the trick, says, Why these bonds? Loose me, ye swains, and hear the song which you desire :—

*Tum vero in numerum Faunosque ferasque videres
Ludere, tum rigidas motare cacumina quercus.*
ECL. vi. l. 27.

*Music has charms to soothe the savage breast,
To soften rocks, and bend the knotted oak.*
DRYDEN.

MARCH 26.
1785.

CONTENTS.

A.
	Page
AT the sign of the horse	12
As walking forth to view the plain	26
And gin ye meet a bonny lassie	29
All in the downs	76
A cobler there was	85
As you mean to set sail	152
Adieu, ye groves, adieu ye plains	187
A pox of your pother,	189
Ah! Chloris	196
As down on Banna's banks	216
As Jamie Gay	221
All you who would wish to succeed	223
Assist me ye lads	233
A lass that was laden'd with care	260
All you that are wife, and think life	265
At setting day, and rising morn	292

B.
Believe my sighs, my tears, my dear	116
Blyth, blyth, blyth, was she	133
By the gaily circling glass	177
Beneath a green shade	268
Blow high, blow low	328

C.
Contented I am, and contented	38
Come, come, my jolly lads	41
Cease rude Boreas	109
Come rouse brother sportsmen	164
Come, come, my brave tars	251
Come gie's a sang the lady cry'd	278
Come all ye young lovers	322
Curtis was old Hoge's wife	332

CONTENTS.

D.
	Page
Down the burn Davie	1
Dear Tom, this brown jug	53
Dear Kathleen you no doubt	145
Dear Roger if your Jenny geck	274
De'el take the wars	340

E.
Ev'ry man take his glass in his hand	67

F.
For lake of gold	8
For me, my fair, a wreath	20
Fill your glasses	31
Farewell to Lochaber	43
Free from the bustle, care, and strife	227
Fine songsters apologies too often use	229
Four and twenty fidlers all on a row	240
From the east breaks the morn	244
From Roslin castle's echoing walls	302
Farewell, ye green fields	325

G.
Gin I had a wee house	205
Gallant sailor, oft you told me	295

H.
Here awa, there awa,	17
Hark away, 'tis the merry ton'd horn	37
Hark! hark! the joy inspiring horn	71
How little do the landmen know	125
How stands the glass around	146
Had I heart for falsehood fram'd	217
Had Neptune, when first he took	286
Hear me, ye nymphs, and every swain,	290
How happy's he	346

I.
I'll never leave thee	3
I'm not high church, nor low church	87

CONTENTS.

	Page
I figh and lament me in vain	94
I'ts open the door fome pity to fhow	101
If I live to grow old	104
Ianthe the lovely	112
I'm in love with twenty	128
In the garb of old Gaul	178
In winter when the rain rain'd cauld	193
If to force me to fing, it be your intention	212
In April when primrofes	282
Jove in his chair	344

L.

Laft time I came o'er the muir	5
Let a fet of fober affes	49
Life is checquer'd	114
Let gay ones and great	246

M.

My temples with clufters	121
My daddy is a canker'd carle	123
My Patie is a lover gay	182
My fond fhepherds	191
My love was once a bonny lad	253
My fheep I've forfaken	292
Man may efcape from rope or gun	313
My laddie is gone far awa o'er the plain	334

N.

Now Phœbus gilds the orient fkies	140
Now fmiling fpring again appears	259
No more my fong fhall be, ye fwains	311

O.

O Beffy Bell and Mary Gray	7
On Etrick Banks	15
O faw ye my father	25
Once more I'll tune the vocal fhell	81
On a bank of flowers	83
O thou lov'd country	92
O what had I ado for to marry	140

CONTENTS.

	Page
O sweet Sir, for your courtesie	159
O greedy Midas, I've been told	161
O I hae lost my silken snood	163
Old women we are,	166
O what pleasures will abound	169
One morning very early	214
O send Lewis Gordon hame	277
O late in an ev'ning forth I went	317

P.
Proud Paris, despising fair Helen's great pomp	289

R.
Rail no more, ye learned asses	246

S.
Songs of shepherds, in rustical roundelays	53
Shepherds, I have lost my love	75
Says Colin to me, I've a thought in my head	129
Since you mean to hire for service	175
Sweet Annie frae the sea beach came	185
Some talk of Alexander, and some of Hercules	231
Says Plato, why should man be vain	255
Such beauties in view	270

T.
The last time I came o'er the muir	5
To Anacreon in heav'n	22
The women all tell me I'm false to my lass	47
There was a jolly miller once	61
The dusky night rides down the sky	62
The topsails shiver in the wind	73
The echoing horn	88
The moon had climb'd the highest hill	96
The night her silent sable wore	98
The wheel of life	108
'Twas I learnt a pretty song in France	130
The smiling morn	135
The wealthy fool with gold in store	137
Tho' late I was plump, round, and jolly	139

CONTENTS.

	Page
The man that's contented is void of all care	149
There was a little man	154
The lawland lads think they are fine	170
There liv'd a man in Baleno crazy	203
The fields were green	224
Thro' the fiery flames of love	235
The lafs of Peatie's mill	242
The plowman he's a bonny lad	248
'Twas fummer, and foftly	262
The whiftling plowman	266
'Twas within a mile of Edinburgh town	272
This cold flinty heart	275
The world, my dear Myra	296
'Twas in that feafon of the year	301
The wand'ring failor plows the main	308
The charge it prepar'd	324
Thurfday in the morn	330
Tho' wifdom will preach about joys, Sir	326

W.

When the fheep are in the fauld	10
Will ye go the ew-bughts, Marion	33
What fports can compare	35
When I was a young one	45
When war's alarms	51
Whence comes it, neighbour Dick	55
What is't to us who guides the ftate	65
When once the gods, like us below	78
What woman can do	90
When my locks are grown hoary	102
Where-ever I'm going, and all the day long	107
Welcome, welcome, brother debtor	120
Where's my fwain fo blythe and clever	126
When merry hearts were gay	156
Why heaves my fond bofom	173
When late I wander'd o'er the plain	206
When Britain firft at heav'n's command	208
When earth's foundation firft was laid	211
Whatever fqueamifh lovers may fay	218
What beauties does Flora difclofe	236

CONTENTS.

	Page
When Maggy and I fell acquaint	239
When I was in my fe'enteen years	256
When firſt my dear laddie	284
We're gaily yet, and we're gaily yet	288
When firſt I came to be a man	304
When I have a faxpence under my thumb	320

Y.

Ye lads of true fpirit, pay courtſhip to claret	18
Ye belles, and ye flirts	68
You know I'm your prieſt	105
You the point may carry	118
Ye ſluggards, who murder your lifetime in ſleep	200
Ye ſportſmen draw near	314

THE MUSICAL MISCELLANY.

SONG I.
DOWN THE BURN DAVIE.

When trees did bud, and fields were green, And broom bloom'd fair to see; When Mary was complete fifteen, And love laugh'd in her ee': Blyth Davie's blinks her heart did move, To speak her mind thus free; Gang down the burn, Davie love, And I will fol - - - low thee.

A

Now Davie did each lad furpafs
  That dwelt on this burn fide;
And Mary was the bonnieft lafs,
  Juft meet to be a bride.
    Blyth Davie's blinks, &c.

Her cheeks were rofy, red and white,
  Her ee'n were bonny blue,
Her looks were like Aurora bright,
  Her lips like dropping dew.
    Blyth Davie's blinks, &c.

What pafs'd, I guefs, was harmlefs play,
  And nothing, fure, unmeet!
For, ganging hame, I heard them fay,
  They lik'd a walk fo fweet.
    Blyth Davie's blinks, &c.

His cheeks to her's he fondly laid;
  She cry'd, " Sweet love be true;
" And when a wife, as now a maid,
  " To death I'll follow you."
    Blyth Davie's blinks, &c.

As fate had dealt to him a routh,
  Straight to the kirk he led her;
There plighted her his faith and truth,
  And a bonny bride he made her.
No more afham'd to own her love,
  Or fpeak her mind thus free;
" Gang down the burn, Davie, love,
  " And I will follow thee."

SONG II.
I'LL NEVER LEAVE THEE.

One day I heard Mary say, How shall I leave thee. Stay dearest Ado-nis, stay, Why wilt thou grieve me. A-las my fond heart will break, If thou should leave me, I'll live and die for thy sake, Yet ne---ver leave thee.

Say, lovely Adonis, say,
  Has Mary deceiv'd thee.
Did e'er her young heart betray
  New love to grieve thee.

A ij

My conſtant mind ne'er ſhall ſtray,
  Thou may believe me ;
I'll love thee, lad, night and day,
  And never leave thee.

Adonis, my charming youth,
  What can relieve thee.
Can Mary thy anguiſh foothe.
  This breaſt ſhall receive thee.
My paſſion can ne'er decay,
  Never deceive thee :
Delight ſhall drive pain away,
  Pleaſure revive thee.

But leave thee, leave thee, lad,
  How ſhall I leave thee.
O ! that thought makes me ſad.;
  I'll never leave thee.
Where would my Adonis fly ;
  Why does he grieve me.
Alas ! my poor heart will die,
  If I ſhould leave thee.

SONG III.
LAST TIME I CAME O'ER THE MUIR.

Beneath the cooling ſhade we lay,
   Gazing and chaſtely ſporting ;
We kiſs'd and promis'd time away,
   Till night ſpread her black curtain.
I pitied all beneath the ſkies,
   Even kings, when ſhe was nigh me ;
In raptures I beheld her eyes,
   Which cou'd but ill deny me.

Shou'd I be call'd where cannons roar,
   Where mortal ſteel may wound me ;
Or caſt upon ſome foreign ſhore,
   Where dangers may ſurround me ;
Yet hopes again to ſee my love,
   To feaſt on glowing kiſſes,
Shall make my care at diſtance move,
   In proſpect of ſuch bliſſes.

In all my ſoul there's not one place
   To let a rival enter ;
Since ſhe excels in every grace,
   In her my love ſhall center.
Sooner the ſeas ſhall ceaſe to flow,
   Their waves the Alps to cover ;
On Greenland's ice ſhall roſes grow,
   Before I ceaſe to love her.

The next time I gang o'er the muir,
   She ſhall a lover find me ;
And that my faith is firm and pure,
   Tho' I left her behind me :
Then Hymen's ſacred bonds ſhall chain
   My heart to her fair boſom ;
There, while my being does remain,
   My love more freſh ſhall bloſſom.

SONG IV.
BESSY BELL AND MARY GRAY.

O Bef·fy Bell and Mary Gray, They war' twa bonny laſ-ſes, They bigg'd a bow'r on yon burn brae, And theek'd it o'er wi' ra--ſhes. Fair Beſ--fy Bell I loo'd yeſtreen, And thought I ne'er cou'd alter; But Mary Gray's twa pawky een, They gar my fan-cy fal-ter.

Now Beſſy's hair's like a lint-tap;
  She ſmiles like a May morning,
When Phœbus ſtarts frae Thetis' lap,
  The hills with rays adorning:
White is her neck, ſaft is her hand,
  Her waiſt and feet's fu' genty;
With ilka grace ſhe can command;
  Her lips, O vow! they're dainty.

And Mary's locks are like a craw,
  Her een like diamonds glances;
She's ay ſae clean, redd up, and braw,
  She kills whene'er ſhe dances:
Blyth as a kid, with wit at will,
  She blooming, tight, and tall is;
And guides her airs ſae gracefu' ſtill,
  O Jove, ſhe's like thy Pallas.

Dear Beſſy Bell and Mary Gray,
  Ye unco fair oppreſs us;
Our fancies jee between you tway,
  Ye are ſic bonny laſſes:
Waes me! for baith I canna get,
  To ane by law we're ſtented;
Then I'll draw cuts, and tak' my fate,
  And be with ane contented.

SONG V.

FOR LAKE OF GOLD.

For lake of gold ſhe's left me O! And of
all that's dear bereft me O! She me for-

No cruel fair shall ever move
My injur'd heart again to love;
Through distant climates I must rove,
　Since Jeany she has left me.
Ye pow'rs above, I to your care
Give up my charming lovely fair;
Your choicest blessings be her share,
　Tho' she's for ever left me.

SONG VI.
AULD ROBIN GRAY.

When the sheep are in the fauld, and the ky at hame, And a' the warld to sleep are gane, The waes of my heart fa's in show'rs frae my ee', When my gudeman lies found by me.

Young Jamie loo'd me well, and he sought me for his bride,
But saving a crown, he had naething beside;
To make that crown a pound, my Jamie went to sea,
And the crown and the pound were baith for me.

He hadna' been awa' a week but only twa,
When my mither she fell sick, and the cow was stown'n awa';
My father brake his arm, and my Jamie at the sea,
And auld Robin Gray came a-courting me.

My father cou'dna' wirk, and my mither cou'dna' fpin,
I toil'd day and night, but their bread I cou'dna' win;
Auld Rob maintain'd them baith, and wi' tears in his ee',
Said, Jenny, for their fakes, O marry me.

My heart it faid na', I look'd for Jamie back,
But the wind it blew high, and the fhip it was a wreck;
The fhip it was a wreck, why didna' Jenny die,
And why do I live to cry, *Waes me!*

Auld Robin argu'd fair, tho' my mither didna' fpeak,
She look'd in my face, till my heart was like to break;
So they gied him my hand, tho' my heart was in the fea,
And auld Robin Gray is gudeman to me.

I hadna' been a wife a week but only four,
When, fitting fae mournfully at the door,
I faw my Jamie's wreath, but didna' think it he,
Till he faid, I'm come back for to marry thee.

O fair did we greet, and muckle did we fay,
We took but ae kifs, and we tore ourfelves away;
I wifh I were dead, but I'm no like to die,
And why do I live to fay, *Waes me!*

I gang like a ghaift, and carena' to fpin,
I darena' think on Jamie, for that wou'd be a fin;
But I'll do my beft, a gude wife to be,
For auld Robin Gray is kind to me.

SONG VII.

THE VICAR AND MOSES.

At the sign of the horse, old Spintext of course, Each night took his pipe and his pot, O'er a jorum of nappy, quite pleasant and happy, Was plac'd this canonical sot. *Tol de rol de rol ti-dol di dol.*

The evening was dark, when in came the clark,
    With reverence due and submission;
First strok'd his cravat, then twirl'd round his hat,
    And bowing, preferr'd his petition.

I'm come, Sir, says he, to beg look, d'ye see,
    Of your reverend worship and glory,
To inter a poor baby, with as much speed as may be,
    And I'll walk with the lanthorn before you.

The body we'll bury, but pray where's the hurry?
  Why Lord, Sir, the corpſe it does ſtay:
You fool hold your peace, ſince miracles ceaſe,
  A corpſe, Moſes, can't run away.

Then Moſes he ſmil'd, ſaying, Sir, a ſmall child
  Cannot long delay your intentions;
Why that's true, by St Paul, a child that is ſmall,
  Can never enlarge it's dimenſions.

Bring Moſes ſome beer, and bring me ſome, d'ye hear,
  I hate to be call'd from my liquor:
Come, Moſes, The King, 'tis a ſcandalous thing,
  Such a ſubject ſhould be but a Vicar.

Then Moſes he ſpoke, Sir 'tis paſt twelve o'clock,
  Beſides there's a terrible ſhower;
Why Moſes, you elf, ſince the clock has ſtruck twelve,
  I'm ſure it can never ſtrike more.

Beſides, my dear friend, this leſſon attend,
  Which to ſay and to ſwear I'll be bold,
That the corpſe, ſnow or rain, can't endanger, that's plain,
  But perhaps you or I may take cold.

Then Moſes went on, Sir the clock has ſtruck one,
  Pray maſter look up at the hand;
Why it ne'er can ſtrike leſs, 'tis a folly to preſs
  A man for to go that can't ſtand.

At length, hat and cloak old Orthodox took,
  But firſt cram'd his jaw with a quid;
Each tipt off a gill, for fear they ſhould chill,
  And then ſtagger'd away ſide by ſide.

When come to the grave, the clerk hum'd a ſtave,
  Whilſt the ſurplice was wrapt round the Prieſt;
Where ſo droll was the figure of Moſes and Vicar,
  That the pariſh ſtill talk of the jeſt.

B

Good people, let's pray, put the corpfe t'other way,
 Or perchance I fhall over it ftumble;
'Tis beft to take care, tho' the fages declare,
 A *mortuum caput* can't tremble.

Woman that's born of a man, that's wrong, the leaf's torn;
 O man, that is born of a woman,
Can't continue an hour, but is cut down like a flow'r;
 You fee, Mofes, death fpareth no man.

Here, Mofes, do look, what a confounded book,
 Sure the letters are turn'd upfide down.
Such a fcandalous print, fure the devil is in't,
 That this Bafket fhould print for the Crown.

Prithee, Mofes, you read, for I cannot proceed,
 And bury the corpfe in my ftead.
  (Amen. Amen.)
Why, Mofes, your're wrong, pray hold ftill your tongue,
 You've taken the tail for the head.

O where's thy fting, Death! put the corpfe in the earth,
 For, believe me, 'tis terrible weather.
So the corpfe was interr'd, without praying a word.
 And away they both ftagger'd together,
  Singing *Tol de rol de rol ti dol di dol.*

SONG VIII.

ON ETRICK BANKS.

On Etrick banks, ae summer's night, at gloming when the sheep drave hame, I met my lassie braw and tight, Came wading barefoot, a' her lane: My heart grew light, I ran, I flang My arms about her lil - - ly neck, And kiss'd and clap'd her there fu' lang, My words they were na mony feck.

I faid, My laffie, will ye go
    To the Highland hills, the Earfe to learn,
I'll baith gi'e thee a cow and ew,
    When ye come to the brigg of Earn.
At Leith auld meal comes in, ne'er fafh,
    And herrings at the Broomielaw.
Chear up your heart, my bonny lafs,
    There's gear to win we never faw.

All day when we have wrought enough,
    When winter, frofts and fnaw begin,
Soon as the fun gaes weft the loch,
    At night when ye fit down to fpin,
I'll fcrew my pipes and play a fpring:
    And thus the weary night we'll end,
Till the tender kid and lamb-time bring
    Our pleafant fummer back again.

Syne when the trees are in their bloom,
    And gowans glent o'er ilka field,
I'll meet my lafs amang the broom,
    And lead you to my fummer fhield.
Then far frae a' their fcornfu din,
    That make the kindly hearts their fport
We'll laugh and kifs, and dance and fing,
    And gar the langeft day feem fhort.

SONG IX.

HERE AWA, THERE AWA.

Through the lang muir I have follow'd my Willie,
Through the lang muir I have follow'd him hame,
Whate'er betide us, nought shall divide us;
Love now rewards all my forrow and pain.

Here awa, there awa, here awa, Willie;
Here awa, there awa, here awa hame;
Come love, believe me, naething can grieve me,
Ilka thing pleafes while Willie's at hame.

B iij

SONG X.
YE LADS OF TRUE SPIRIT.

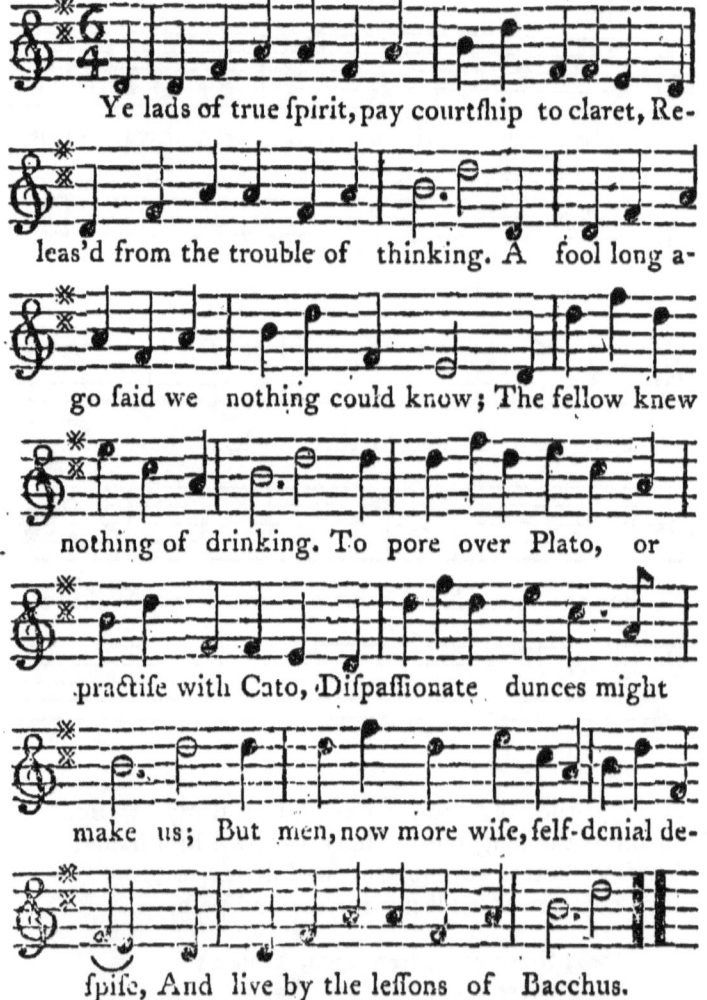

Ye lads of true spirit, pay courtship to claret, Releas'd from the trouble of thinking. A fool long ago said we nothing could know; The fellow knew nothing of drinking. To pore over Plato, or practise with Cato, Difpaffionate dunces might make us; But men, now more wife, felf-denial defpife, And live by the leffons of Bacchus.

Big-wig'd, in fine coach, fee the doctor approach;
   He folemnly up the ftair paces;
Looks grave—fmells his cane—applies finger to vein,
   And counts the repeats with grimaces.

As he holds pen in hand, life and death are at stand—
   A toss up which party shall take us.
Away with such cant—no prescription we want
   But the nourishing nostrum of Bacchus.

We jollily join in the practice of wine,
   While misers 'midst plenty are pining;
While ladies are scorning, and lovers are mourning,
   We laugh at wealth, wenching, and whining.
Drink, drink, now 'tis prime; toss a bottle to Time,
   He'll not make such haste to o'ertake us;
His threats we prevent, and his cracks we cement,
   By the styptical balsam of Bacchus.

What work is there made, by the newspaper-trade,
   Of this man's and t'other man's station!
The inns are all bad, and the outs are all mad;
   In and out is the cry of the nation.
The politic patter which both parties chatter
   From bumpering freely shan't shake us;
With half-pints in hand, independent we'll stand
   To defend Magna Charta of Bacchus.

Be your motion's well-tim'd; be all charg'd and all prim'd;
   Have a care—right and left—and make ready.
Right hand to glass join—at your lips rest your wine;
   Be all in your exercise steady.
Our levels we boast when our women we toast;
   May graciously they undertake us!
No more we desire—so drink and give fire,
   A volley to beauty and Bacchus!

SONG XI.
FOR ME MY FAIR.

For me my fair a wreath has wove, where rival

flow'rs in union meet, where rival flow'rs in union

meet; As oft she kifs'd this gift of love, her

breath gave fweetnefs to the fweet, as oft she kifs'd the

gift of love, her breath gave fweetnefs to the fweet,

her breath gave fweetnefs to the fweet.

A bee within a damaſk roſe
  Had crept, the nectar'd dew to ſip,
But leſſer ſweets the thief forgoes,
  And fixes on Louiſa's lip.

There taſting all the bloom of ſpring,
  Wak'd by the rip'ning breath of May,
Th' ungrateful ſpoiler left his ſting,
  And with the honey fled away.

SONG XII.
TO ANACREON IN HEAVEN.

To Anacreon in heav'n, where he fat in full glee,

A few fons of harmony fent a petition, That he

their infpirer and patron would be; When this

anfwer arriv'd from the jolly old Grecian—Voice

fiddle, and flute, No longer be mute, I'll lend

you my name and infpire you to boot; And befides

I'll inftruct you like me to intwine The myrtle of

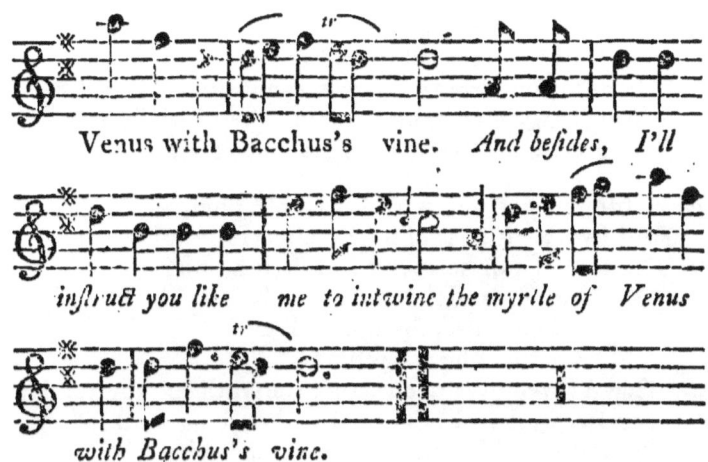

Venus with Bacchus's vine. *And besides, I'll instruct you like me to intwine the myrtle of Venus with Bacchus's vine.*

The news through Olympus immediately flew;
  When old Thunder pretended to give himself airs—
" If these mortals are suffer'd their scheme to pursue,
  " The devil a goddess will stay above stairs.
    " Hark! already they cry,
    " In transports of joy,
  " Away to the sons of Anacreon we'll fly,
" And there, with good fellows, we'll learn to intwine
" The myrtle of Venus with Bacchus's vine.

" The yellow-hair'd God and his nine fusty maids,
  " From Helicon's banks will incontinent flee,
" Idalia will boast but of tenantless shades,
  " And the bi-forked hill a mere defart will be.
    " My thunder, no fear on't,
    " Shall soon do it's errand,
  " And, dam'me! I'll swinge the ringleaders, I warrant,
" I'll trim the young dogs, for thus daring to twine
" The myrtle of Venus with Bacchus's vine."

Apollo rose up; and said, " Pr'ythee ne'er quarrel,
  " Good king of the Gods, with my vot'ries below:
" Your thunder is useless"—then, shewing his laurel,
  Cry'd, " *Sic evitabile fulmen*, you know!

" Then over each head
　　　" My laurels I'll spread ;
　　　" So my sons from your crakers no mischief shall dread,
　　" Whilst snug in their club-room, they jovially twine
　　" The myrtle of Venus with Bacchus's vine.

Next Momus got up, with his risible phiz,
　And swore with Apollo he'd chearfully join—
" The tide of full harmony still shall be his,
　　" But the song, and the catch, and the laugh shall be mine.
　　" Then, Jove, be not jealous
　　　" Of these honest fellows,"
　　Cry'd Jove, "We relent, since the truth you now tell us;
" And swear, by old Styx, that they long shall intwine
" The myrtle of Venus with Bacchus's vine."

Ye sons of Anacreon, then, join hand in hand ;
　Preserve unanimity, friendship, and love ;
'Tis your's to support what's so happily plann'd ;
　You've the sanction of Gods, and the fiat of Jove.
　　　While thus we agree,
　　　Our toast let it be.
　May our club flourish happy, united, and free !
And long may the sons of Anacreon intwine
The myrtle of Venus with Bacchus's vine.

SONG XIII.

O SAW YE MY FATHER.

Up Johnny rose, and to the door he goes,
    And gently tirled the pin.
The laſſie taking tent, unto the door ſhe went,
    And ſhe open'd and let him in.

Flee up, flee up, my bonny grey cock,
    And craw when it is day;
Your neck ſhall be like the bonny beaten góld,
    And your wings of the ſilver grey.

The cock prov'd falſe, and untrue he was,
    For he crew an hour o'er ſoon.
The laſſie thought it day when ſhe ſent her love away,
    And it was but a blink of the moon.

SONG XIV.
KATHARINE OGIE.

I stood a while, and did admire,
To see a nymph so stately;

So brisk an air there did appear
  In a country-maid so neatly?
Such natural sweetness she display'd,
  Like a lillie in a boggie.
Diana's self was ne'er array'd
  Like this same Katharine Ogie.

The flow'r of females, beauty's queen,
  Who sees thee, sure must prize thee;
Though thou art dress'd in robes but mean,
  Yet these cannot disguise thee;
Thy handsome air, and graceful look,
  Far excels any clownish rogie;
Thou'rt match for laird, or lord, or duke,
  My charming Katharine Ogie.

O were I but some shepherd swain!
  To feed my flock beside thee,
At bughting-time to leave the plain,
  In milking to abide thee;
I'd think myself a happier man.
  With Kate, my club, and dogie,
Than he that hugs his thousands ten,
  Had I but Katharine Ogie.

Then I'd despise th' imperial throne,
  And statesmens dangerous stations:
'd be no king, I'd wear no crown,
  I'd smile at conqu'ring nations:
Might I caress and still possess
  This lass of whom I'm vogie,
For these are toys, and still look less,
  Compar'd with Katharine Ogie.

But I fear the gods have not decreed
  For me so fine a creature,
Whose beauty rare makes her exceed
  All other works in nature.
Clouds of despair surround my love,
  That are both dark and foggy:
Pity my case ye powers above,
  Else I die for Katharine Ogie.

SONG XV.

FY GAR RUB HER O'ER WI' STRAE.

Sweet youth's a blyth and heartsome time;
   Then, lads and lasses, while 'tis May,
Gae pu' the gowan in it's prime,
   Before it wither and decay.

Watch the faft minutes of delyte,
   When Jenny fpeaks beneath her breath,
And kiffes, laying a' the wyte
   On you, if fhe kepp ony fkaith.

Haith ye're ill-bred, fhe'll fmiling fay,
   Ye'll worry me, ye greedy rook:
Syne frae your arms fhe'll rin away,
   And hid herfelf in fome dark nook.
Her laugh will lead you to the place,
   Where lies the happinefs ye want,
And plainly tell you to your face,
   Nineteen na-fays are ha'f a grant.

Now to her heaving bofom cling,
   And fweetly toolie for a kifs:
Frae her fair finger whoop a ring,
   As taiken of a future blifs.
Thefe bennifons, I'm very fure,
   Are of the gods indulgent grant:
Then, furly carls, whifht, forbear
   To plague us with your whining cant.

SONG XVI.

FILL YOUR GLASSES.

Fill your glasses banish grief, Laugh and worldly

care despise; Sorrow ne'er will bring relief: Joy from

drinking will arise. Why should we, with wrinkl'd care

Change what nature made so fair? Drink, and set the

heart at rest; Of a bad market make the best.

Busy brains we know, alas!
   With imaginations run;
Like the sands i' th' hour-glass,
   Turn'd and turn'd, and still run on,
Never knowing where to stay,
But uneasy ev'ry way.
Drink, and set the heart at rest;
Peace of mind is always best.

Some pursue the winged wealth,
    Some to honours high aspire:
Give me freedom, give me health;
    There's the sum of my desire.
What the world can more present
Will not add to my content,
Drink, and set the heart at rest;
Peace of mind is always best.

Mirth, when mingled with our wine,
    Make the heart alert and free;
Should it snow, or rain, or shine,
    Still the same thing 'tis with me.
There's no fence against our fate;
Changes daily on us wait.
Drink, and set your hearts at rest;
Of a bad market make the best.

SONG XVII.
EW-BUGHTS MARION.

Will ye go to the ew bughts Marion, And wear in the sheep wi' me? The sun shines sweet, my Marion, But nae half sae sweet as thee. The sun shines sweet, my Marion, But nae half sae sweet as thee.

O Marion's a bonny lafs,
    And the blyth blinks in her ee';
And fain wad I marry Marion,
    Gin Marion wad marry me.

There's goud in your garters, Marion,
    And filk on your white haufs-bane;
Fu' fain wad I kifs my Marion,
    At e'en when I come hame.

I've nine milks ewes, my Marion;
  A cow and a brawny quey,
I'll gi'e them a' to my Marion;
  Juft on her bridal-day;

And ye's get a green fey apron,
  And waftecoat of the London brown,
And vow but ye will be vap'ring,
  Whene'er ye gang to the town.

I'm young and ftout, my Marion;
  Nane dances like me on the green:
And gin ye forfake me, Marion,
  I'll e'en draw up wi' Jean;

Sae put on your pearlins, Marion,
  And kyrtle of the cramafie!
And foon as my chin has nae hair on,
  I fhall come weft, and fee ye.

MISCELLANY. 35

SONG XVIII.

HUNTING THE HARE.

What sport can compare, to the hunting of the

hare, In the morning, In the morning, In fair and

pleasant weather, With our horses and our hounds,

we will scour o'er the grounds, and Tan-ta-ra, Huz-

za, and Tan-ta-ra, Huz-za and Tan-ta-ra, Huz-

za, brave boys we will follow.

When poor puss doth rise,
Then away from us she flies,
And we give her a thundering hollow,

With our horſes and our hounds
We will pull her courage down,
And Tantara, Huzza, brave boys we will follow.

When poor puſs is kill'd
We retire from the field,
To be merry boys, and drink away all ſorrow,
We have nothing more to fear
But to drown old father Care,
And to baniſh, Huzza, all his wants till to-morrow.

SONG XIX.

HARK AWAY.

Hark a-way 'tis the merry ton'd horn, Calls the hunters all up with the morn, To the hills and the woodlands we steer, To unharbour the out lying deer And all the day long this this is our song, still hollowing and following so frolic and free. Our joys know no bounds while we're af-ter the hounds, No mortals on earth are so jol-ly as we.

Round the woods when we beat how we glow,
While the hills they all echo Hollow!
With a bounce from his cover the ſtag flies,
Then our ſhouts long refound thro' the ſkies.
  Chorus. And all the day long, &c.

When we ſweep o'er the valleys, or climb
Up the health breathing mountain ſublime,
What a joy from our labours we feel,
Which alone they who taſte can reveal.
  Chorus. And all the day long, &c.

SONG XX.
CONTENTED I AM.

Contented I am, and contented I'll be, For what can
this world more afford, Than a laſs who will ſociably
ſit on my knee, And a cellar with liquor well
ſtor'd, My brave bo - - - - - - - - - ys, And a cellar
with liquor well ſtor'd,

My vault door is open, defcend and improve;
  That cafk, fir, ay, that we will try;
'Tis as rich to the tafte as the lips of your love,
  And as bright as her cheeks to the eye.

In a piece of flit hoop fee my candle is ftuck;
  'Twill light us the bottle to hand,
The foot of my glafs for the purpofe I broke,
  For I hate that a bumper fhould ftand.

Sound thefe pipes, they're in tune; fearch the bins, they're
    well fill'd;
  View that heap of old hock in the rear.
Yon bottles are Burgundy; mark how they're pil'd,
  Like artillery, tier over tier.

My cellar's my camp; my foldiers my flafks,
  All glorioufly rang'd in review;
When I caft my eyes round, I confider my cafks
  As kingdoms I've yet to fubdue.

Like Macedon's madman, my glafs I'll enjoy,
  Defying hyp, gravel, or gout.
He cry'd when he had no more worlds to deftroy:
  I'll weep when my liquor is out.

'Tis my will, when I die not a tear fhall be fhed,
  No HIC JACET be cut on my ftone;
But pour on my coffin a bottle of red,
  And fay that his drinking is done.

D ij

SONG XXI.

THE HOUNDS ARE ALL OUT.

To the foregoing Tune.

THE hounds are all out and the morning does peep,
    Why how now you fluggardly fot !
How can you, how can you lie fnoring a-afleep,
    While we all on horfeback have got my brave boy.
    While we all on horfeback have got.

I cannot get up, for the over night's cup,
    So terribly lies in my head,
Befides my wife cries, my dear do not rife,
    But cuddle me longer a-bed my dear boy.
    But cuddle me longer a-bed.

Come on with your boots, and faddle your mare,
    Nor tire us with your longer delay,
The cry of the hounds, and the fight of the hare,
    Will chafe all our vapours away my brave boys.
    Will chafe all our vapours away.

SONG XXII.
COME, COME, MY JOLLY LADS.

Come come, my jolly lads, the wind's abaft, brisk gales our sails shall croud, Come bustle, bustle, bustle boys, hawl the boat, the boatswain pipes a-loud; The ship's unmoor'd, all hands on board, The rising gale fills ev'ry sail the ship's well mann'd and stor'd. Then fling the flowing bowl, Fond hopes arise, the girls we prize shall bless each jovial soul. The cann boys bring, we'll drink and sing while foaming billows roll.

Tho' to the Spanish coast
  We're bound to steer,
We'll still our rights maintain,
Then bear a hand, be steady boys,
  Soon we'll see
Old England once again:
  From shore to shore,
  While cannons roar,
Our tars shall show
The haughty foe,
  Britannia rules the main.

Then fling the flowing bowl,
  Fond hopes arise
  The girls we prize
Shall bless each jovial soul:
  The cann boys bring,
  We'll drink and sing,
While foaming billows roll.

Cho. Then fling the, &c.

SONG XXIII.
LOCHABER NO MORE.

Farewell to Lochaber! and farewell my Jean! where heartsome with thee I have mony days been; For, Lochaber no more, Lochaber no more, We'll may be return to Lochaber no more. These tears that I shed, they are a' for my dear, And no for the dangers attending on weir; Tho' bore on rough seas to

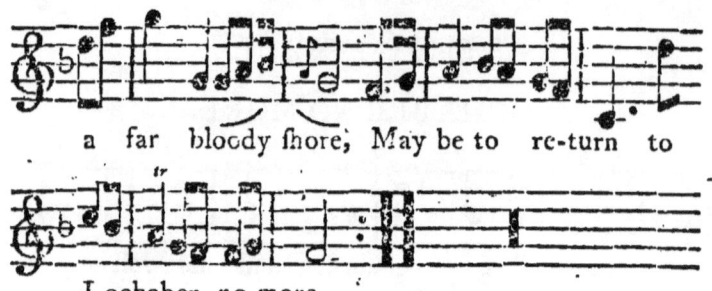

a far bloody shore; May be to return to Lochaber no more.

Tho' hurricanes rise, and rise every wind,
They'll ne'er make a tempest, like that in my mind :
Tho' loudest of thunders on louder waves roar,
That's naething like leaving my love on the shore.
To leave thee behind me, my heart is fair pain'd,
By ease that's inglorious, no fame can be gain'd.
And beauty and love's the reward of the brave :
And I must deserve it, before I can crave.

Then glory, my Jeany, maun plead my excuse,
Since honour commands me, how can I refuse?
Without it I ne'er can have merit for thee,
And without thy favour I'd better not be.
I gae then, my lass, to win honour and fame.
And if I should luck to come gloriously hame.
I'll bring a heart to thee with love running o'er,
And then I'll leave thee and Lochaber no more.

SONG XXIV.

WHEN I WAS A YOUNG ONE.

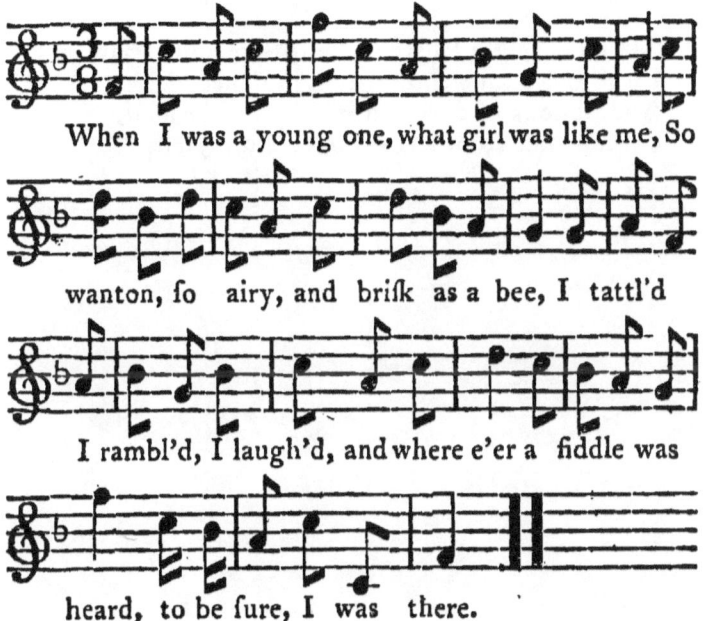

When I was a young one, what girl was like me, So

wanton, fo airy, and brifk as a bee, I tattl'd

I rambl'd, I laugh'd, and where e'er a fiddle was

heard, to be fure, I was there.

To all that come near I had fomething to fay,
'Twas this Sir, and that Sir! but fcarce ever nay,
And Sundays dreft out in my filks and my lace,
I warrant I ftood by the beft in the place.

At twenty, I got me a hufband—poor man!
Well reft him—we all are as good as we can;
Yet he was fo peevifh, he'd quarrel for ftraws,
And jealous—tho' truly I gave him fome caufe.

He fnub'd me and huff'd me—but let me alone,
Egad I've a tongue—and I paid him his own;
Ye wives take the hint and when fpoufe is untowr'd,
Stand firm to our charter—and have the laft word.

But now I'm quite alter'd, the more to my woe,
I'm not what I was forty fummers ago;
This Time's a fore foe, there's no fhunning his dart;
However I keep up a pretty good heart.

Grown old, yet I hate to be fitting mum chance,
I ftill love a tune tho' unable to dance.
And, books of devotion laid by on the fhelf,
I teach that to others—I once did myfelf.

SONG XXV.
THE WOMEN ALL TELL ME.

'The women all tell me I'm falſe to my laſs; That I

quit my poor Chloe, and ſtick to my glaſs. But to

you, men of reaſon, my reaſons I'll own; And if you

don't like them, why let them alone.

Although I have left her, the truth I'll declare;
I believe ſhe was good, and I'm ſure ſhe was fair;
But goodneſs and charms in a bumper I ſee
That make it as good and as charming as ſhe.

My Chloe had dimples and ſmiles, I muſt own;
But, though ſhe could ſmile, yet in truth ſhe could frown;
But tell me, ye lovers of liquor divine,
Did you e'er ſee a frown in a bumper of wine?

Her lillies and roſes were juſt in their prime;
Yet lillies and roſes are conquer'd by time:
But, in wine, from it's age ſuch benefit flows,
That we like it the better the older it grows.

They tell me my love would in time have been cloy'd,
And that beauty's infipid when once 'tis enjoy'd;
But in wine I both time and enjoyment defy,
For, the longer I drink, the more thirfty am I.

Let murders, and battles, and hiftory, prove
The mifchiefs that wait upon rivals in love;
But in drinking, thank heav'n, no rival contends,
For, the more we love liquor, the more we are friends.

She too might have poifon'd the joy of my life,
With nurfes, and babies, and fqualling and ftrife;
But my wine neither nurfes or babies can bring,
And a big-bellied bottle's a mighty good thing.

We fhorten our days when with love we engage;
It brings on difeafes and haftens old age:
But wine from grim death can it's votaries fave.
And keep out t'other leg when there's one in the grave.

Perhaps, like her fex, ever falfe to their word,
She has left me—to get an eftate, or a lord;
But my bumpers (regarding nor titles nor pelf)
Will ftand by me when I can't ftand by myfelf.

Then let my dear Chloe no longer complain:
She's rid of her lover, and I of my pain;
For in wine, mighty wine, many comforts I fpy.—
Should you doubt what I fay, take a bumper and try.

SONG XXVI.
LET A SET OF SOBER ASSES.

round.

The ancient sects on happiness
  All differ'd in opinion;
    But wiser rules
    Of Modern schools
In wine fix her dominion.
    Power and wealth, &c.

Wine gives the lover vigour,
  Makes glow the cheeks of beauty;
    Makes poets write,
    And foldiers fight,
And friendfhip do it's duty.
  Power and wealth, &c.

Wine was the only Helicon
  Whence poets are long-liv'd fo;
    'Twas no other main
    Than brifk champaign
Whence Venus was deriv'd too.
  Power and wealth, &c.

When heaven in Pandora's box
  All kind of ill had fent us,
    In a merry mood
    A bottle of good
Was cork'd up to content us.
  Power and wealth, &c.

All virtues wine is nurfe to,
  Of ev'ry vice deftroyer;
    Give dullards wit,
    Makes juft the cit,
Truth forces from the lawyer.
  Power and wealth, &c.

Wine fets our joys a-flowing,
  Our care and forrow drowning.
    Who rails at the bowl,
    Is a Turk in's foul,
And a Chriftian ne'er fhould own him.
  Power and wealth, &c.

SONG XXVII.
WHEN WARS ALARMS.

When wars alarms entic'd my Willy from me, My poor heart with grief did sigh, Each fond re- membrance brought fresh sorrow on me, I woke e'er yet the morn was nigh. No other could delight him, ah why did I e'er slight him? Coldly answ'ring his fond tale, Which drove him far Amidst the rage of war, And left silly me thus to bewail.

But I no longer, tho' a maid forsaken,
   Thus will mourn like yonder dove,
For, 'ere the lark to-morrow shall awaken,
   I will seek my absent love;
   The hostile country over
   I'll fly to seek my lover,
Scorning ev'ry threat'ning fear;
   Nor distant shore,
   Nor cannon's roar,
Shall longer keep me from my dear.

SONG XXVIII.
DEAR TOM.

Dear Tom, this brown jug, that now foams with mild ale, (in which I will drink to sweet Nan of the vale), Was once Toby Filpot, a thirsty old soul As e'er drank a bottle or fathom'd a bowl. In boozing about 'twas his praise to excel, And among jolly topers he bore off the bell, - - - - - - - - - - - - - - - - - he bore off the bell.

It chanc'd as in dog-days he sat at his ease,
In his flow'r-woven arbour, as gay as you please,
With a friend and a pipe puffing sorrow away,
And with honest old Stingo was soaking his clay,
His breath-doors of life on a sudden were shut.
And he dy'd full as big as a Dorchester butt.

His body, when long in the ground it had lain,
And time into clay had resolv'd it again,
A potter found out in it's covert so snug,
And with part of fat Toby he form'd this brown jug.
Now sacred to friendship, to mirth, and mild ale;
So here's to my lovely sweet Nan of the vale.

SONG XXIX.
HAPPY DICK.

Whence comes it, neighbour Dick, That you with youth uncommon, Have serv'd the girls this tri - - - - ck, And wedded an old wo - - - man? Happy Dick!

Each belle condemns the choice
   Of a youth so gay and sprightly;
But we, your friends, rejoice,
   That you have judg'd so rightly:
Happy Dick!

Though odd to some it sounds,
   That on threescore you ventur'd,
Yet in ten thousand pounds
   Ten thousand charms are center'd:
Happy Dick!

Beauty, we know will fade,
   As doth the short liv'd flower;
Nor can the fairest maid
   insure her bloom an hour:
Happy Dick!

Then wifely you refign,
   For fixty, charms fo tranfient;
As the curious value coin
   The more for being ancient:
Happy Dick!

With joy your fpoufe fhall fee
   The fading beauties round her,
And fhe herfelf ftill be
   The fame that firft you found her:
Happy Dick!

Oft is the married ftate
   With jealoufies attended;
And hence, through foul debate,
   Are nuptial joys fufpended:
Happy Dick?

But you, with fuch a wife,
   No jealous fears are under;
She's yours alone, for life,
   Or much we all fhall wonder:
Happy Dick!

Her death would grieve you fore,
   But let not that torment you;
My life! fhe'll fee fourfcore,
   If that will but content you:
Happy Dick!

On this you may rely,
   For the pains you took to win her,
She'll ne'er in child-bed die,
   Unlefs the d—l's in her:
Happy Dick!

Some have the name of hell
   To matrimony given:
How falfely you can tell,
   Who find it fuch a heaven:
Happy Dick!

With you, each day and night
  Is crown'd with joy and gladnefs;
While envious virgins bite
  The heated fheets for madnefs:
Happy Dick!

With fpoufe long fhare the blifs
  Y'had mifs'd in any other;
And when you've bury'd this,
  May you have fuch another:
Happy Dick!

Obferving hence, by you,
  In marriage fuch decorum,
Our wifer youth fhall do
  As you have done before 'em:
Happy Dick!

SONG XXX.

HOW NOW MADAM FLIRT.

To the foregoing Tune.

WHY how now, madam Flirt;
  If you thus muft chatter,
And are for flinging dirt,
  Let's try who beft can fpatter;
         Madam Flirt!
Why how now, faucy jade;
  Sure the winch is tipfy!
How can you fee me made
  The fcoff of fuch a gipfy?
         Saucy Jade?

SONG XXXI.
SONGS OF SHEPHERDS.

Not too fast.

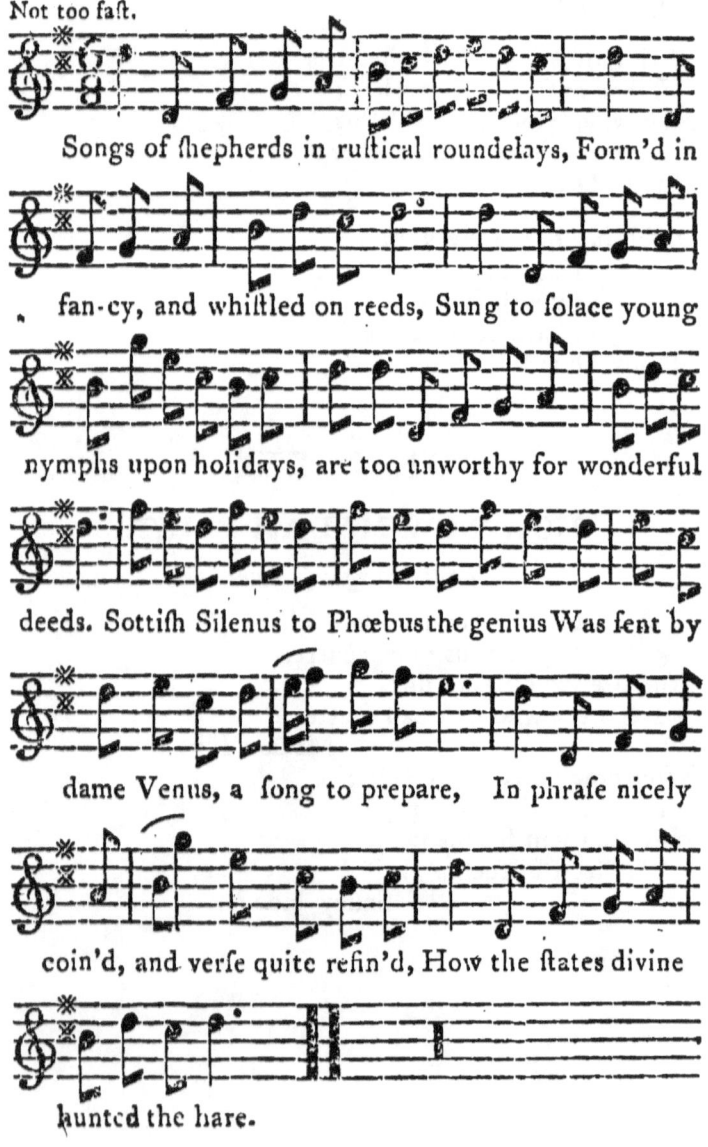

Songs of shepherds in rustical roundelays, Form'd in fan-cy, and whittled on reeds, Sung to solace young nymphs upon holidays, are too unworthy for wonderful deeds. Sottish Silenus to Phœbus the genius Was sent by dame Venus, a song to prepare, In phrase nicely coin'd, and verse quite refin'd, How the states divine hunted the hare.

Stars quite tired with paſtimes Olympical.
  Stars and planets that beautiful ſhone,
Could no longer endure that men only ſhould
  Revel in pleaſures, and they but look on.
Round about horned Lucina they ſwarmed,
  And quickly inform'd her how minded they were,
Each god and goddeſs to take human bodies,
  As lords and ladies, to follow the hare.

Chaſte Diana applauded the motion,
  And pale Proſerpina ſat down in her place,
To guide the welkin and govern the ocean,
  While Dian conducted her nephews in chace.
By her example, their father to trample,
  The earth old and ample, they ſoon leave the air:
Neptune the water, and wine Liber pater,
  And Mars the ſlaughter, to follow the hare.

Young god Cupid was mounted on Pegaſus,
  Borrow'd o' th' muſes with kiſſes and prayers;
Stern Alcides upon cloudy Caucaſus
  Mounted a centaur that proudly him bears.
The poſtilion of the ſky, light-heel'd ſir Mercury,
  Made his ſwift courſer fly fleet as the air;
While tuneful Apollo the paſtime did follow,
  To whoop and to hollow, boys, after the hare.

Drowned Narciſſus, from his metamorphoſis
  Rous'd by Echo, new manhood did take.
Snoring Somnus upſtarted from Cim'ries:
  Before for a thouſand years he did not wake.
There was lame club-footed Mulciber booted;
  And Pan, too, promoted on Corydon's mare.
Eolus flouted; with mirth Momus ſhouted;
  While wife Pallas pouted, yet follow'd the hare.

Grave Hymen uſhers in lady Aſtrea.
  The humour took hold of Latona the cold.
Ceres the brown too, with bright Cytherea,
  And Thetis the wanton, Bellona the bold;

Shamefac'd Aurora with witty Pandora,
  And Maia with Flora did company bear;
But Juno was flated too high to be mated,
  Although, Sir, she hated not hunting the hare.

Three brown bowls of Olympical nectar
  The Troy-born boy now prefents on his knee;
Jove to Phœbus caroufes in nectar,
  And Phœbus to Hermes, and Hermes to me:
Wherewtih infufed, I piped and mufed,
  In language unufed, their fports to declare,
Till the vaft houfe of Jove like the bright fpheres did move.
  Here's a health, then, to all that love hunting the hare.

SONG XXXII.
THERE WAS A JOLLY MILLER.

There was a jolly miller once liv'd on the river Dee. He danc'd and he sang from morn till night; no lark so blithe as he. And this the burden of his song for ever us'd to be: I care for nobody, no, not I, if nobody cares for me.

I live by my mill, God bless her! she's kindred, child, and wife;
I would not change my station for any other in life.
No lawyer, surgeon, or doctor, e'er had a groat from me
I care for nobody, no, not I, if nobody cares for me.
When spring begins it's merry career, oh! how his heart grows gay!
No summer's drouth alarms his fears, nor winter's sad decay,
No foresight mars the miller's joy, who 's wont to sing and say,
Let others toil from year to year, I live from day to day.
Thus, like the miller bold and free, let us rejoice and sing:
The days of youth are made for glee, and time is on the wing.
This song shall pass from me to thee, along this jovial ring:
Let heart and voice and all agree to say long live the king.

SONG XXXIII.
THE DUSKY NIGHT.

The duſky night rides down the ſky, And uſhers in the morn, The hounds all join in jovial cry, The hounds all join in jovial cry, The huntſman winds his horn. The huntſman winds his horn. And a hunting we will go, A hunting we will go, A hunting we will go - - -, A hunting we will go And a hunting we will go. A hunting we

will go - -, And hunting we will go - - -, A hunting we will go

The wife around her huſband throws
   Her arms to make him ſtay,
My dear it rains, it hails, it blows,
   You cannot hunt to-day.
     Yet a hunting, &c.

Sly Reynard now like light'ning flies,
   And ſweeps acroſs the vale,
But when the hounds too near he ſpies
   He drops his buſhy tail.
     Then a hunting, &c.

Fond eccho ſeems to like the ſport,
   And join the jovial cry,
The woods and hills the ſound retort,
   And muſic fills the ſky,
     When a hunting, &c.

At laſt his ſtrength to faintneſs worn,
   Poor Reynard ceaſes flight ;
Then hungry homeward we return
   To feaſt away the night.
     And a drinking, &c.

Ye jovial hunters in the morn
   Prepare then for the chace.
Riſe at the ſounding of the horn,
   And health with ſport embrace,
     When a hunting, &c.

SONG XXXIV.

FATHER PAUL.

To the foregoing Tune.

WHILE grave divines preach up dull rules,
  And moral wits refine,
The precepts taught in human fchools,
The precepts taught in human fchools,
  We Friars hold divine,
  We Friars hold divine.
    Here's a health to Father Paul,
    A health to Father Paul;
    For flowing bowls inspires the fouls
    Of jolly Friars all.

When in the convent we're all met,
  We laugh, we joke, we fing,
Affairs divine, we foon forget,
Affairs divine, we foon forget,
    Since Father Paul's our King,
    Since Father Paul's our King.
      Here's a health, &c.

Our beads and crofs, we hold divine
  We pray with fervent zeal,
To rofy Bacchus god of wine,
To rofy Bacchus god of wine,
  Who does each joy reveal,
  Who does each joy reveal,
      Here's a health, &c.

Here's abfolution you'll receive,
  You blue eye'd nuns fo fair,
And benediction we will give,
And benediction we will give,
    So banifh all your cares,
    So banifh all your cares,
      Here's a health, &c.

MISCELLANY.

So fill your bumpers sons of mirth,
  Let Friars be the toast;
Long may they all exist on earth,
Long may they all exist on earth,
  And nuns their order boast,
  Aud nuns their order boast,
    Here's a health, &c.

SONG XXXV.
WHAT IS'T TO US.

What is't to us who guides the state? Who's out of favour, or who's great? Who are the ministers or spies? Who votes for places, or who buys? Who are the mini - sters or spies? Who votes for places, or who buys?

F iij

The world will still be rul'd by knaves,
And fools contending to be slaves;
Small things, my friend, serve to support
Life, troublesome at best, and short.

Our youth runs back, occasion flies,
Grey hairs come on, and pleasure dies;
Who would the present blessing lose
For empire which he cannot use?

Kind providence has us supply'd
With what to others is deny'd;
Virtue which teaches to condemn
And scorn ill actions and ill men.

Beneath this lime-tree's fragrant shade,
On beds of flow'rs supinely laid,
Let's, then, all other cares remove,
And drink and sing to those we love.

SONG XXXVI.
EV'RY MAN TAKE HIS GLASS.

Ev'ry man take his glafs in his hand, And drink a good health to our king; Many years may he rule o'er this land; May his laurels for ever frefh fpring. Let wrangling and jangling ftraitway ceafe; Let every man ftrive for his country's peace; Neither tory nor whig With their parties look big: Here's a health to all honeft men.

'Tis not owning a whimſical name
  That proves a man loyal and juſt :
Let him fight for his country's fame ;
  Be impartial at home, if in truſt.
'Tis this that proves him an honeſt ſoul :
His health we'll drink in a brim-full bowl.
    Then let's leave off debate,
    No confuſion create :
Here's a health to all honeſt men.

When a company's honeſtly met,
  With intent to be merry and gay,
Their drooping ſpirits to whet,
  And drown the fatigues of the day,—
What madneſs is it thus to diſpute,
When neither ſide can his man confute ?
    When you've ſaid what you dare,
    You're but juſt where you were.
Here's a health to all honeſt men.

Then agree, ye true Britons, agree,
  And ne'er quarrel about a nick-name ;
Let your enemies trembling ſee
  That a Briton is always the ſame.
For our king, our laws, our church, and right,
Let's lay by all feuds and ſtraite unite :
    Then who need care a fig
    Who's a tory or whig ?
Here's a health to all honeſt men.

SONG XXXVII.

YE BELLES AND YE FLIRTS.

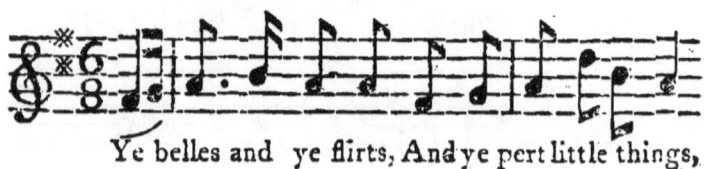

Ye belles and ye flirts, And ye pert little things,

MISCELLANY.

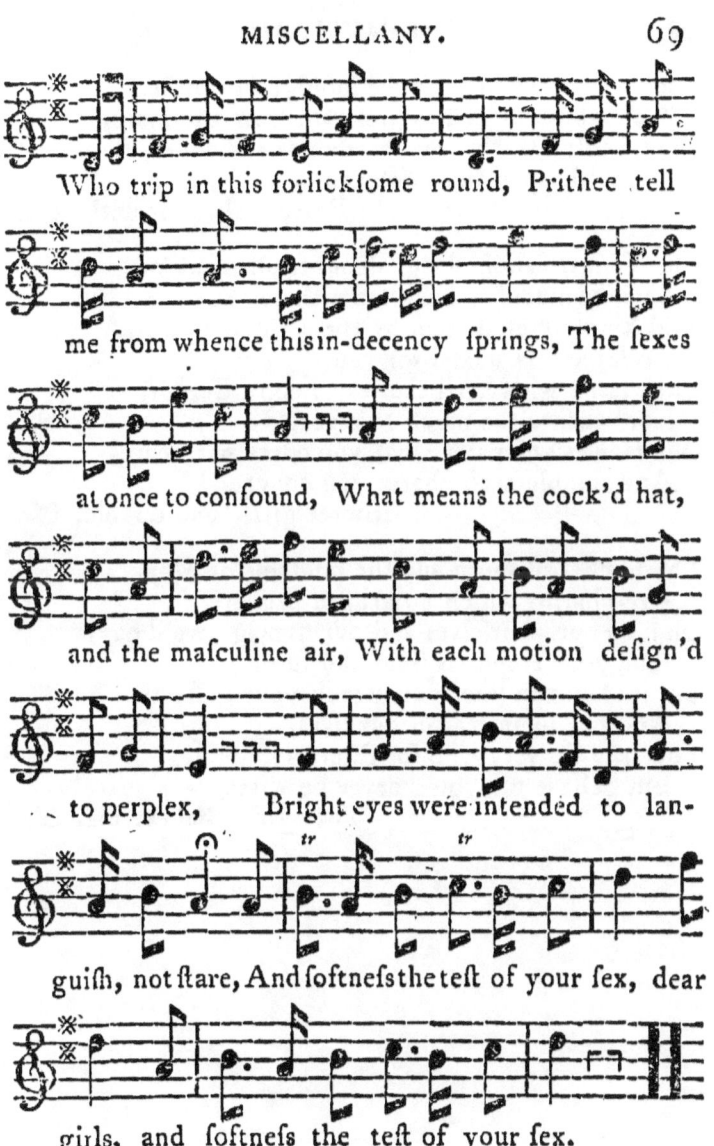

Who trip in this forlicksome round, Prithee tell me from whence this in-decency springs, The sexes at once to confound, What means the cock'd hat, and the masculine air, With each motion design'd to perplex, Bright eyes were intended to languish, not stare, And softness the test of your sex, dear girls, and softness the test of your sex.

The girl who on beauty depends for support,
   May call ev'ry art to her aid,
The bosom display'd, and the petticoat short,
   Are samples she gives of her trade,

But you, on whom fortune indulgently fmiles,
  And whom pride has preferv'd from the fnare,
Should flily attack us with coynefs and wiles,
  Not with open and infolent airs,
            Brave girls, not with, &c.

The Venus, whofe ftatue delights all mankind,
  Shrinks modeftly back from the view,
And kindly fhou'd feem by the artift defign'd,
  To ferve as a model for you,
Then learn with her beauties to copy her air,
  Nor venture too much to reveal,
Our fancies will paint what you cover with care,
  And double each charm you conceal,
            Sweet girls, and double, &c.

The blufhes of morn and the mildnefs of May,
  Are charms which no art can procure,
Oh! be but yourfelves and our homage we'll pay,
  And your empire is folid and fure,
But if Amazon like, you attack your gallants,
  And put us in fear of our lives,
You may do very well for fifters and aunts,
  But believe me you'll never be wives,
            Poor girls, believe me, &c.

SONG XXXVIII.
HARK! HARK!

Hark! hark! the joy in-fpi-ring horn, Salutes the ro-fy ri-fing morn, And e-choes thro' the dale ---- And e-choes thro' the dale, With clam'rous peals the hills refound, The hounds quick fcented fcow'r the ground, And fnuff the fragrant gale --- And fnuff the fragrant gale.

Nor gates nor hedges can impede,
The brisk high-mettl'd starting steed,
   The jovial pack pursue;
Like light'ning darting o'er the plains,
The distant hills with speed he gains,
   And sees the game in view.

Her path the timid hare forsakes,
And to the copse for shelter makes,
   There pants a while for breath;
When now the noise alarms her ear,
Her haunt's descry'd' her fate is near,
   She sees aproaching death.

Directed by the well-known breeze,
The hounds their trembling victim seize,
   She faints, she falls, she dies;
The distant coursers now come in,
And join the loud triumphant din,
   Till eccho rend the skies.

SONG XXXIX.
TOPSAILS SHIVER IN THE WIND.

The topsails shi - - ver in the wind, The ship she casts to sea - - - But yet my soul, my heart, my mind, are, Ma - ry, moor'd with thee. For tho' thy sailor's bound a - far, still love shall be his leading star; For tho' thy sailor's bound a - - far, Still love shall be his lead - - ing star.

G

Should landmen flatter when we're fail'd,
 O doubt their artful tales;
No gallant sailor ever fail'd,
 If love breath'd conſtant gales:
Thou art the compaſs of my ſoul
Which ſteers my heart from pole to pole.

Sirens in every port we meet,
 More fell than rocks or waves;
But ſuch as grace the Britiſh fleet,
 Are lovers and not ſlaves:
No foes our courage ſhall ſubdue,
Although we've left our hearts with you.

Theſe are our cares, but if you're kind,
 We'll ſcorn the daſhing main,
The rocks, the billows, and the wind,
 The pow'r of France and Spain:
Now England's glory reſts with you,
Our ſails are full, ſweet girls, Adieu!

SONG XL.

BANKS OF BANNA.

Shepherds, I have loft my love, Have you feen my Anna? Pride of ev'ry fhady grove, Upon the banks of Banna. I for her my home forfook, near yon mifty mountains, Left my flock, my pipe, my crook, Greenwood fhade and fountain.

Never fhall I fee them more
  Until her returning;
All the joys of life are o'er,
  From gladnefs chang'd to mourning.
Whither is my charmer flown?
  Shepherds tell me whither?
Ah, woe for me, perhaps fhe's gone
  For ever and for ever.

SONG XLI.
ALL IN THE DOWNS.

All in the Downs the fleet was moor'd, the ſtreamers waving to the wind, When black ey'd Suſan came on board, Oh! where ſhall I my true love find; Tell me, ye jovial ſailors, tell me true, If my ſweet William, if my ſweet Willi - am, ſails a - mong your crew.

William, who high upon the yard,
    Rock'd with the billows to and fro,
Soon as her well known voice he heard,
    He sigh'd and cast his eyes below:
The cord glides swiftly thro' his glowing hands,
And quick as light'ning on the deck he stands.

So the sweet lark, high pois'd in air,
    Shuts close his pinions to his breast,
If chance his mate's shrill call he hear,
    And drops at once into her nest,
The noblest captain in the British fleet,
Might envy William's lips those kisses sweet.

O Susan, Susan, lovely dear,
    My vows shall ever true remain;
Let me kiss off that falling tear,
    We only part to meet again,
Change as ye list, ye winds, my heart shall be,
The faithful compass that still points to thee.

Believe not what the landmen say,
    Who tempt with doubts thy constant mind,
They'll tell thee sailors when away,
    In ev'ry port a mistress find;
Yes, yes, believe them when they tell thee so,
For thou art present wheresoe'er I go.

If to far India's coast we sail,
    Thy eyes are seen in diamonds bright,
Thy breath is Africk's spicy gale,
    Thy skin is ivory so white;
Thus ev'ry beauteous object that I view,
Wakes in my soul some charm of lovely Sue.

Though battle calls me from thy arms,
    Let not my pretty Susan mourn;
Though cannons roar, yet safe from harms,
    William shall to his dear return,

Love turns afide the balls that round me fly,
Left precious tears fhould drop from Sufan's eye.

The boatfwain gave the dreadful word,
　　The fails their fwelling bofom fpread,
No longer muft fhe ftay aboard:
　　They kifs'd, fhe figh'd, he hung his head,
Her lefs'ning boat, unwilling rows to land:
Adieu, fhe cries, and wav'd her lily hand.

SONG XLII.

WHEN ONCE THE GODS.

When once the gods, like us below, To keep it up

de - fign, Their goblets with frefh nectar flow, Which

makes them more divine. Since drinking de-i-fies

the foul, Let's pufh a - bout the flowing bowl,

The glittring ſtar and ribbon blue,
  That deck the courtier's breaſt,
May hide a heart of blackeſt hue,
  Though by the king careſs'd.
Let him in pride and ſplendor roll;
We'er happier o'er a flowing bowl.
  A flowing bowl, &c.

For liberty let patriots rave,
  And damn the courtly crews
Becauſe, like them, they want to have
  The loaves and fiſhes too.

I care not who divides the cole,
So I can ſhare a flowing bowl.
   A flowing bowl, &c.

Let Mansfield Lord-chief-juſtice be,
   Sir Fletcher ſpeaker ſtill;
At home let Sandwich rule the ſea,
   And North the treaſury fill:
No place I want, throughout the whole,
But one that's near a flowing bowl.
   A flowing bowl, &c.

The ſon wants ſquare-toes at old Nick,
   And miſs is mad to wed;
The doctor wants us to be ſick;
   The undertaker, dead.
All have their wants from pole to pole;
I want an ever flowing bowl.
   A flowing bowl, &c.

MISCELLANY. 81

SONG XLIII.
ONCE MORE I'LL TUNE.

The fun firſt riſing in the morn,
That paints the dew beſpangled thorn,
Does not ſo much the day adorn,
    As does my lovely Peggy.

And when in Thetis lap to reft,
He ftreaks with gold the ruddy weft,
He's not fo beauteous, as undrefs'd
    Appears my lovely Peggy.

Were fhe array'd in ruftic weed,
With her the bleating flocks I'd feed,
And pipe upon mine oaten reed,
    To pleafe my lovely Peggy.
With her a cottage would delight,
All's happy when fhe's in my fight,
But when fhe's gone it's endlefs night,
    All's dark without my Peggy.

The zephyr's air the violet blows,
Or breath upon the damafk rofe,
He does not half the fweets difclofe,
    That does my lovely Peggy.
I ftole a kifs the other day,
And truft me, nought but truth I fay,
The fragrant breath of blooming May,
    Was not fo fweet as Peggy.

While bees from flow'r to flow'r fhall rove,
And linnets warble thro' the grove,
Or ftately fwans the waters love,
    So long fhall I love Peggy.
And when Death with his pointed dart,
Shall ftrike the blow that rives my heart,
My words fhall be when I depart,
    Adieu! my lovely Peggy.

MISCELLANY. 83

SONG XLIV.

ON A BANK OF FLOW'RS.

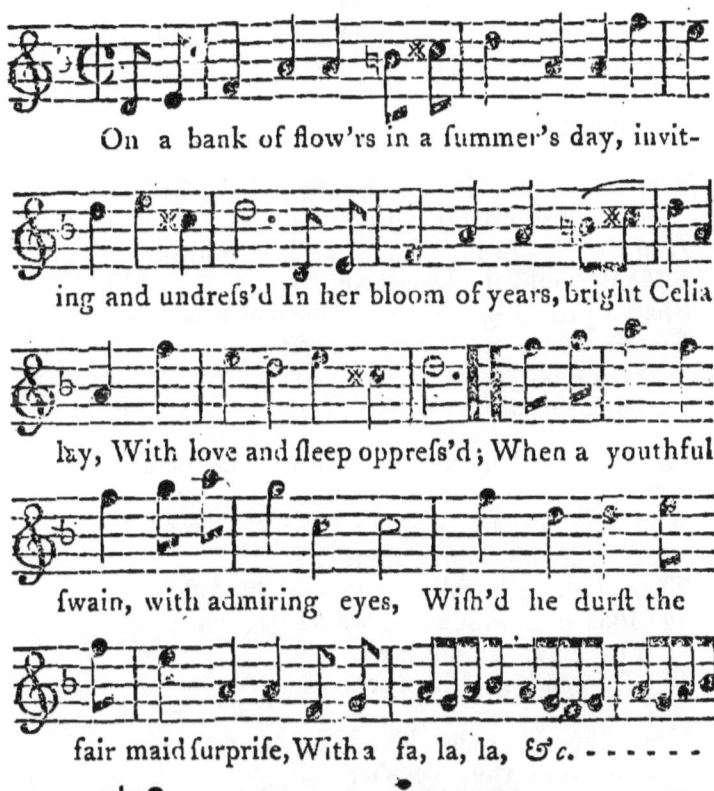

On a bank of flow'rs in a summer's day, invit-

ing and undress'd In her bloom of years, bright Celia

lay, With love and sleep oppress'd; When a youthful

swain, with admiring eyes, Wish'd he durst the

fair maid surprise, With a fa, la, la, &c. - - - - - -

But fear'd approaching spies.

As he gaz'd, a gentle breeze arose,
   That fann'd her robes aside;
And the sleeping nymph did charms disclose
   Which, waking, she would hide,
Then his breath grew short, and his pulse beat high,
He long'd to touch what he chanc'd to spy,
   With a fa, la, la, &c.
But durst not yet draw nigh.

All amaz'd he flood, with her beauties fir'd,
  And blefs'd the courteous wind;
Then in whifpers figh'd, and the gods defir'd,
  That Celia might be kind.
Then, with hope grown bold, he advanc'd amain:
But fhe laugh'd aloud in a dream, and again,
  With a fa, la, la, &c.
Repell'd the tim'rous fwain.

Yet, when once defire has enflam'd the foul,
  All modeft doubts withdraw,
And the god of love does each fear controul
  That would the lover awe.
Shall a prize like this, fays the vent'rous boy,
Efcape, and I not the means employ,
  With a fa, la, la, &c.
To feize the proffer'd joy?

Here the glowing youth, to relieve his pain,
  The flumb'ring maid carefs'd,
And with trembling hands (oh! the fimple fwain!)
  Her glowing bofom prefs'd.
Then the virgin wak'd, and affrighted flew,
Yet look'd as wifhing he would purfue,
  With a fa, la, la, &c.
But Damon mifs'd his cue.

Now, repenting that he had let her fly,
  Himfelf he thus accus'd:
What a dull and ftupid thing was I,
  That fuch a chance abus'd!
To my fhame 'twill now on the plains be faid,
Damon a virgin afleep betray'd,
  With a fa, la, la, &c.
Yet let her go a maid!

SONG XLV.

A COBLER THERE WAS.

A cobler there was, And he liv'd in a stall, Which

serv'd him for parlour, for kitchen, and hall. No

coin in his pocket, no care in his pate; No ambition had

he, nor yet duns at his gate. Derry down, down,

down, derry down.

Contented he work'd, and he thought himself happy
If at night he could purchase a cup of brown nappy:
He'd laugh, then, and whistle, and sing, too, most sweet,
Saying, just to a hair I've made both ends to meet.
    Derry down, &c.

But love, the disturber of high and of low,
That shoots at the peasant as well the beau,
He shot the poor cobler quite thorough the heart;
I wish'd it had hit some more ignoble part.
    Derry down, &c.

It was from a cellar this archer did play,
Where a buxom young damfel continually lay :
Her eyes fhone fo bright, when fhe rofe ev'ry day,
That fhe fhot the poor cobler quit over the way.
    Derry down, &c.

He fang her love-fongs as he fat at his work,
But fhe was as hard as a Jew or a Turk ;
Whenever he fpoke fhe would flounce and would fleer,
Which put the poor cobler quite into defpair.
    Derry down, &c.

He took up his AWL that he had in the world,
And to make away with himfelf he refolv'd :
He peirc'd through his body inftead of the SOLE ;
So the cobler he dy'd, and the bell it did toll.
    Derry down, &c.

And now, in good will, I advife, as a friend :
All coblers, take notice of this cobler's END ;
Keep your hearts out of love, for we find, by what's paft,
That love brings us all to an END at the LAST.
    Derry down, down, down, derry down.

SONG XLVI.

To the foregoing Tune.

I'M not high church nor low church, no tory nor whig,
   No flattering young coxcomb, nor formal old prig,
Not fond of much talking, nor silently quaint,
No profligate sinner, nor pragmatical saint.
    Derry down, down, down, derry down.

But to know truth from falsehood, I do what I can,
And if that I do err, I'm a fallible man,
Nor can I in nature conceive any other,
Of the wisest arch priest that is born of his mother.

I can laugh at a jest, if it's not out of time,
And excuse a mistake, tho' not flatter a crime
The faults of a friend I scorn to expose,
And detest private scandal, tho' cast on my foes.

I put none to the blush, on whatever pretence,
For immodesty shocks both good breeding and sense,
To amend, not reproach, is the bent of my mind,
A reproof is half lost, where ill nature is join'd.

When merit appears, tho' in rags, I respect it,
And pleads virtue's cause, tho' the world should reject it;
To no party a slave, in no squabble I join,
Nor damns the opinion that differs from mine,

Evil tongues I contemn, no mob treason I sing,
I doat on my country, and am true to my king,
And as for the path, after death to be trode,
I submit to the will of a merciful God.
    Derry down, down, down, derry down.

SONG XLVII.
THE ECHOING HORN.

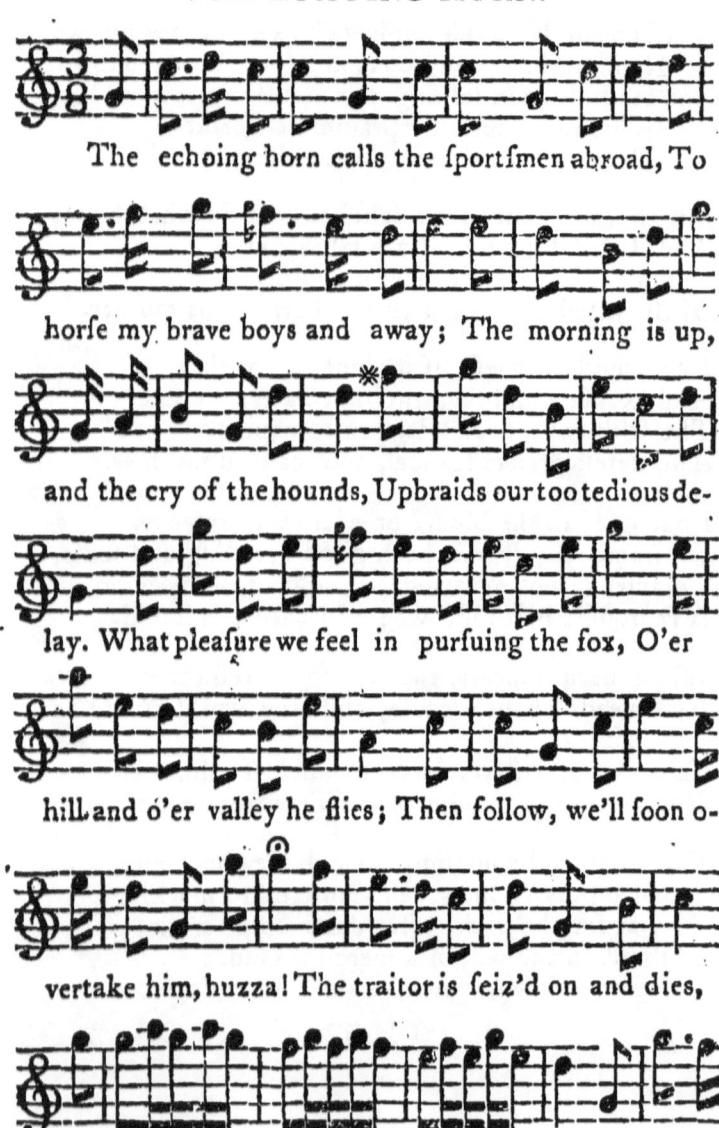

The echoing horn calls the sportsmen abroad, To horse my brave boys and away; The morning is up, and the cry of the hounds, Upbraids our too tedious delay. What pleasure we feel in pursuing the fox, O'er hill and o'er valley he flies; Then follow, we'll soon overtake him, huzza! The traitor is seiz'd on and dies, He dies - - - - - - - - - - - - - - The traitor

Chorus.

is seiz'd on and dies; Then follow, we'll soon overtake

him, huzza! The traitor is seiz'd on and dies.

Triumphant returning at night with the spoil,
    Like Bacchanals shouting and gay;
How sweet with a bottle and lass to refresh,
    And lose the fatigues of the day:
With sport, love, and wine, fickle fortune defy,
    Dull wisdom all happiness sours;
Since life is no more than a passage at best,
    Let's strew the way over with flow'rs.
With flow'rs, let's strew, &c.

I caught him once making love to a maid,
    When to him I ran,
He turn'd and he kifs'd me, then who could upbraid
    So civil a man?
The next day I found to a third he was kind,
I rated him foundly, he fwore I was blind;
    So let me do what I can,
        Still,—ftill, he's the man.

All the world bids me beware of his art:
    I do what I can;
But he has taken fuch hold of my heart,
    I doubt he's the man!
So fweet are his kiffes, his looks are fo kind,
He may have his faults, but if none I can find,
    Who can do more than they can?
        He,—ftill is the man.

SONG XLIX.

THE FAREWELL.

Written by MARY QUEEN *of* SCOTS, *in her paſſage from France to Scotland.*

O! thou lov'd country, where my youth was ſpent, Dear golden days all paſt in ſweet content, where the fair morning of my clouded day, Shone mildly bright, and temperately gay, Dear France, adieu, a long and ſad fare-well; No thought can image, And no tongue can tell, The

pangs I feel at that drear word, Farewell!

The ſhip that wafts me from thy friendly ſhore,
    Conveys my body, but conveys no more.
My ſoul is thine, that ſpark of heav'nly flame,
    That better portion of my mingled frame,
Is wholy thine, that part I give to thee,
    That in the temple of thy memory,
The other ever may enſhrined be.

SONG L.
QUEEN MARY'S LAMENTATION.

I sigh and lament me in vain, These walls can but e - - cho my moan, A - - las, it in - creases my pain when I think of the days that are gone. Thro' the grate of my prison, I see the birds as they wanton in air, My heart, how it pants to be free, My looks they are wild with de - spair.

Above tho' opprest by my fate,
   I burn with contempt for my foes,
Tho' fortune has alter'd my state
   She ne'er can subdue me to those;
False woman in ages to come,
   Thy malice detested shall be
And when we are cold in the tomb
   Some heart still will sorrow for me.

Ye roofs where cold damps and dismay,
   With silence and solitude dwell,
How comfortless passes the day,
   How sad tolls the evening bell;
The owls from the battlements cry,
   Hollow wind seems to murmur around,
O Mary, prepare thee to die,
   My blood it runs cold at the sound.

SONG LI.
MARY'S DREAM.

The moon had climb'd the high-eſt hill, Which riſes o'er the ſource of Dee, And from the eaſtern ſum-mit ſhed Her ſil-ver light on tow'r and tree; When Mary laid her down to ſleep, Her thoughts on Sandy, far at ſea; When ſoft and low a voice was heard, Say, Mary, weep no more for me.

She from her pillow gently rais'd
　　Her head to aſk, who there might be.
She ſaw young Sandy ſhiv'ring ſtand,
　　With viſage pale and hollow eye;
" O Mary dear, cold is my clay,
　" It lies beneath a ſtormy ſea,
" Far, far from thee, I ſleep in death,
　" So Mary, weep no more for me.

" Three ſtormy nights and ſtormy days
　" We toſs'd upon the raging main:
" And long we ſtrove our bark to ſave,
　" But all our ſtriving was in vain.
" Ev'n then, when horror chil'd my blood,
　" My heart was fill'd with love for thee:
" The ſtorm is paſt, and I at reſt,
　" So Mary, weep no more for me.

". O maiden dear, thyſelf prepare,
　" We ſoon ſhall meet upon that ſhore,
" Where love is free from doubt and care,
　" And thou and I ſhall part no more."
Loud crow'd the cock, the ſhadow fled,
　　No more of Sandy could ſhe ſee;
But ſoft the paſſing ſpirit ſaid,
　" Sweet Mary, weep no more for me"

SONG LII.
SHE ROSE AND LET ME IN.

But she, with accents all divine,
  Did my fond suit reprove;
And while she chid my rash design,
  She but inflam'd my love.
Her beauty oft had pleas'd before,
  While her bright eyes did roll:
But virtue only had the pow'r.
  To charm my very soul.

Then who wou'd cruelly deceive,
  Or from such beauty part !
I lov'd her so, I could not leave
  The charmer of my heart.
My eager fondness I obey'd,
  Resolv'd she should be mine,
Till Hymen to my arms convey'd
  My treasure so divine.

Now happy in my Nelly's love,
  Transporting is my joy ;
No greater blessing can I prove,
  So bless'd a man am I ;
For beauty may a while retain
  The conquer'd flutt'ring heart,
But virtue only is the chain
  Holds never to depart.

MISCELLANY. 101

SONG LIII.

OPEN THE DOOR TO ME, OH!

It's open the door, some pity to show,
It's open the door to me, Oh! Tho' you
have been false, I'll always prove true, So
open the door to me, Oh!

Cold is the blast upon my pale cheek,
But colder your love unto me, Oh!
   Though you have, &c.

She's open'd the door, she's open'd it wide,
She fees his pale corps on the ground, Oh!
   Though you have, &c.

My true love, she cry'd, then fell down by his side,
Never, never to shut again, Oh!
   Though you have, &c.

SONG LIV.
THE MATRON'S WISH.

When my locks are grown hoary, And my visage looks pale, When my forehead has wrinkles, and mine eye-sight does fail, May my words and mine actions be free from all harm, May I have a good husband

Chorus.

to keep my back warm. O the pleasures of youth, they are flow'rs but of May, our life's but a vapour, our bodies but clay, Yet let me live well, tho'

I live but a day.

With a sermon on Sunday, and a Bible of good print;
With a pot on the fire, and good viands in't;
With ale, beer, and brandy, both winter and summer,
To drink to my gossip, and be pledg'd by my cummer,
    The pleasures of, &c.

With pigs and with poulty, and some money in store,
To purchase the needful, and to give to the poor;
With a bottle of Canary, to sip without sin,
And to comfort my daughter whene'er she lies in.
    The pleasures of, &c.

With a bed soft and easy to rest on at night,
With a maid in the morning to rise with the light,
To do her work neatly, and obey my desire,
To make the house clean, and blow up the fire.
    The pleasures of, &c.

With health and content, and a good easy chair;
With a thick hood and mantle, when I ride on my mare.
Let me dwell near my cupboard, and far from my foes,
With a pair of glass eyes to clap on my nose.
    The pleasures of, &c.

And when I am dead, with a sigh let them say,
Our honest old cummer's now laid in the clay:
When young, she was cheerful, no scold, nor no whore;
She assisted her neighbours, and gave to the poor.
    Tho'·the flow'r of her youth in her age did decay,
    Tho' her life like a vapour evanish'd away,
    She liv'd well and happy unto her last day.

SONG LV.
THE OLD MAN'S WISH.
To the foregoing Tune.

IF I live to grow old, as I find I go down,
  Let this be my fate: in a fair country town,
Let me have a warm houfe with a ftone at my gate,
And a cleanly young girl to rub my bald pate.
    May I govern my paffions with an abfolute fway;
    And grow wifer and better as my ftrength wears away,
    Without gout or ftone, by a gentle decay,

In a country town, by a murmuring brook,
With the ocean at diftance, on which I may look;
With a green fpacious plain without hedge or ftile,
And an eafy pad nag to ride out a mile.
    May I govern, &c.

With Horace and Petrarch, and one or two more
Of the beft wits that liv'd in the ages before;
With a difh of roaft mutton, not ven'fon nor teal,
And clean, though coarfe linen at every meal.
    May I govern, &c.

With a pudding on Sundays, and ftout humming liquor,
And remnants of Latin to puzzle the vicar;
With a hidden referve of good Burgundy wine,
To drink the king's health as oft as we dine.
    May I govern, &c.

With a courage undaunted may I face my laft day:
And, when I am dead, may the better fort fay,——
In the morning when fober, in the ev'ning when mellow,
He is gone, and has left not behind him his fellow:
    For he govern'd his paffions with an abfolute fway;
    And grew wifer and better as his ftrength wore away,
    Without gout or ftone, by a gentle decay.

SONG LVI.
KNOW I'M YOUR PRIEST.

You know I'm your priest, and your conscience is mine; But if you grow wicked, 'tis not a good sign: So leave off your raking, and marry a wife, And then my dear Darby, you're settled for life. Sing a Ballina-mona, o - ro, Ballina-mona, o - ro, Ballina-mona, o - ro, A good merry wedding for me.

The banns being publish'd to chapel we go,
The bride and the bridegroom in coats white as snow,
So modest her air and so sheepish your look,
You out with your ring and I pull out with my book.
    Sing, &c.

I thumb out the place, and I then read away,
She blushes at love and she whispers obey,
You take her dear hand to have and to hold,
I shut up my book and I pocket your gold.
    Sing Ballinamona oro.
    That snug little guinea for me.

The neighbours wish joy to the bridegroom and bride,
The pipers before us you march side by side,
A plentiful dinner gives mirth to each face,
The piper plays up, myself I say grace.
    Sing, &c.
    A good wedding dinner for me.

The joke now goes round and the stocking is thrown,
The curtains are drawn and you're both left alone,
'Tis then my good boy I believe you're at home,
And hey for a christening at nine months to come.
    Sing Ballinamona oro,
    A good merry christening for me.

SONG LVII.

BALLINAMONA.

To the foregoing Tune.

WHEREVER I'm going, and all the day long,
    At home and abroad, or alone in a throng,
I find that my paffion's fo lively and ftrong,
That your name, when I'm filent, ftill runs in my fong.
    Sing Balinamona oro, &c.
    A kifs of your fweet lips for me.

Since the firft time I faw you I take no repofe;
I fleep all the day to forget half my woes;
So hot is the flame in my ftomach that glows,
By St. Patrick, I fear it will burn through my clothes.
    Sing Balinamona ora, &c.
    Your pretty black hair for me.

In my confcience I fear I fhall die in my grave,
Unlefs you comply and poor Phelim will fave,
And grant the petition your lover does crave,
Who never was free till you made him your flave.
    Sing Balinamona ora, &c,
    Your pretty black eyes for me.

On that happy day when I make you my bride,
With a fwinging long fword how I'll ftrut and I'll ftride,
With coach and fix horfes with honey I'll ride,
As before you I walk to the church by your fide.
    Sing Balinamona oro, &c.
    Your lily-white fift for me.

SONG LVIII.

THE WHEEL OF LIFE.

The wheel of life is turning quickly round, And

nothing in this world of certainty is found. The

midwife wheels us in, and death wheels us out; Good

lack! good lack! how things are wheel'd about.

Some few aloft on fortune's wheel do go,
And, as they mount up high, the others tumble low;
For this we all agree, that fate at firſt did will
That this great wheel ſhould never once ſtand ſtill.

The courtier turns, to gain his private ends,
'Till he's ſo giddy grown, he quite forgets his friends:
Proſperity oft times deceives the proud and vain,
And wheels ſo faſt, it turns them out again.

Some turn to this, to that, and ev'ry way,
And cheat and ſcrape for what can't purchaſe one poor day:
But this is far below the gen'rous hearted man,
Who lives, and makes the moſt of life he can.

And thus we're wheel'd about in life's short farce,
'Till we at last are wheel'd off in a rumbling hearse:
The midwife wheels us in, and death wheels us out,
Good lack! good lack! how things are wheel'd about.

SONG LIX.

THE STORM.

Cease rude Boreas, blust'ring railer, List ye landsmen, all to me, messmates hear a brother sailor, sing the dangers of the sea, From bounding billows first in motion, when the distant whirlwinds rise; to the tempest troubled ocean, Where the seas contend with skies.

Lively.
Hark! the boatswain hoarsely bawling,—
    By topsail sheets, and haulyards stand!
Down top-gallants quick be hauling!
    Down your stay-sails, hand, boys, hand!
Now it freshens, set the braces;
    Quick the topsail sheets let go;
Luff, boys, luff, don't make wry faces!
    Up your topsails nimbly clew!

Slow.
Now all you on down-beds sporting,
    Fondly lock'd in beauty's arms,
Fresh enjoyments wanton courting,
    Free from all but love's alarms,—
Round us roar the tempest louder;
    Think what fear our mind enthrals;
Harder yet, it yet blows harder;
    No again the boatswain calls:

Quick.
The topsail-yards point to the wind, boys!
    See all clear to reef each course!
Let the fore-sheets go; don't mind, boys,
    Though the weather should be worse.
Fore and aft the sprit-sail yard get;
    Reef the mizen; see all clear:
Hand up! each preventer-brace set;
    Man the fore-yard; cheer, lads, cheer!

Slow.
Now the dreadful thunder's roaring!
    Peals on peals contending clash!
On our heads fierce rain falls pouring!
    In our eyes blue lightnings flash!
One wide water all around us,
    All above us one black sky!
Diff'rent deaths at once surround us.
    Hark! what means that dreadful cry?

Quick.
The foremaſt's gone, cries every tongue out,
  O'er the lee, twelve feet 'bove deck.
A leak beneath the cheſt-tree's ſprung out;
  Call all hands to clear the wreck.
Quick the lanyards cut to pieces!
  Come, my hearts be ſtout, and bold!
Plumb the well, the lake increaſes;
  Four feet water in the hold!

Slow.
While o'er the ſhip wild waves are beating,
  We for wives or children mourn;
Alas! from hence there's no retreating;
  Alas! from hence there's no return.
Still the lake is gaining on us;
  Both chain-pumps are choak'd below,
Heav'n have mercy here upon us!
  For only that can ſave us now!

Quick.
O'er the lee-beam is the land, boys;
  Let the guns o'er-board be thrown;
To the pump come ev'ry hand, boys;
  See our mizen-maſt is gone,
The leak we've found; it cannot pour faſt:
  We've lighten'd her a foot or more;
Up, and rig a jury fore-maſt;
  She rights, ſhe rights, boys! wear off ſhore.

Now once more on joys we're thinking,
  Since kind fortune ſpar'd our lives;
Come the cann, boys, let's be drinking
  To our ſweethearts and our wives.
Fill it up, about ſhip wheel it;
  Cloſe to th' lips a brimmer join.
Where's the tempeſt now; who feels it?
  None! our danger's drown'd in wine!

SONG LX.

IANTHE THE LOVELY.

I-an-the the lovely, the joy of her swain, by

Iphis was lov'd and lov'd Iphis again, She liv'd

in the youth, and the youth in the fair, their pleasure

was equal, and equal their care, no delight no enjoy-

ment their dotage withdrew, but the longer they

liv'd still the fonder they grew, No delight no enjoy-

ment their dotage withdrew, But the longer they liv'd

ſtill the fonder they grew.

A paſſion ſo happy alarm'd all the plain,
Some envy'd the nymph, but more envy'd the ſwain,
Some ſwore 'twou'd be pity their loves to invade,
That the lovers alone for each other were made.
But all, all conſented that none ever knew,
A nymph be more kind, or a ſhepherd ſo true.

Love ſaw them with pleaſure and vow'd to take care,
Of the faithful, the tender the innocent pair,
What either might want he bid either to move,
But they wanted nothing but ever to love.
He ſaid all to bleſs them his god-head cou'd do,
That they ſtill ſhou'd be kind and they ſhould be true.

114 THE MUSICAL

SONG LXI.
LIFE IS CHECQUER'D.

Philosophical.   Jovial.

Life is checquer'd; toil and pleasure Fill up all the various measure. See the crew in flannel jerkins, Drinking, toping flip by firkins; And, as they raise the tip To their hap-py lip, On the deck is heard no o-ther sound, But prithee, Jack, prithee, Dick, pri-thee, Sam, prithee, Tom, Let the cann go round.

Then hark to the boatswains whistle! whistle! Then

MISCELLANY.

hark to the boatfwain's whiftle! whiftle! Buftle,

buftle, buftle, my boy; Let us ftir, let us toil;

But let's drink all the while, For labour's the price of

our joy, For labour's the price of our joy.

Life is cheequer'd; toil and pleafure
Fill up all the various meafure.
Hark! the crew, with fun-burnt faces,
Chanting black-ey'd Sufan's graces:
   And, as they raife their notes
   Through their rufty throats,
On the deck is heard no other found, &c. &c.

Life is cheequer'd; toil and pleafure
Fill up all the various meafure.
Hark! the crew their cares difcarding
With huftle-cap or with chuck-farthing:
   Still in a merry pin,
   Let them lofe or win,
On the deck is heard no other found, &c. &c.

SONG LXII.
BELIEVE MY SIGHS.

Believe my sighs, my tears, my dear, believe a heart you've won; Believe my vows to you sincere, or Jenny, I'm undone. You say I'm fickle, and apt to change, at every face that's new. Of all the girls I ever saw, I ne'er lov'd one like you, I ne'er lov'd one

Chorus.

like you, my dear, I ne'er lov'd one like you;

Of all the girls I ever faw, I ne'er lov'd one like you.

My heart was like a lump of ice,
   Till warm'd by your bright eye:
And then it kindled in a trice,
   A flame that ne'er can die.
Then take and try me, you fhall find
   That I've a heart that's true;
Of all the girls I ever faw,
   I ne'er lov'd one like you,
     I ne'er lov'd one like you my dear,
     I ne'er lov'd one like you,
     Of all the girls I ever faw,
     I ne'er lov'd one like you.

SONG LXIII.
YOU THE POINT MAY CARRY.

You the point may carry, If a-while you tar-ry,

But for you, I tell you true, no you, I'll never

marry. You the point may carry, If a-while you

tarry, But for you, I tell you true, no you, I'll ne-

-ver marry.

Care our fouls difowning,
Punch our forrows drowning,
 Laugh and love
 And ever prove
Joys our wifhes crowning.
Care our, &c.

To the church I'll hand her.
Then thro' the world I'll wander,
 I'll fob and figh
 Until I die
A poor forsaken gander.
To the church, &c.

Each pious priest since Moses,
One mighty truth discloses,
 You're never vex't
 If this his text,
Go fuddle all your noses.
Each pious, &c.

SONG LXIV.
WELCOME BROTHER DEBTOR.
Tune—*Ceafe rude Boreas*—Page 109.

WELCOME, welcome, brother debtor,
   To this poor but merry place,
Where no bailiff, dun, or fetter,
   Dare to fhew a frighful face.
But, kind Sir, as your're a ftranger,
   Down your garnifh you muft lay,
Or your coat will be in danger;
   You muft either ftrip or pay.

Ne'er repine at your confinement
   From your children or your wife:
Wifdom lies in true refinement,
   Through the various fcenes of life,
Scorn to fhew the leaft refentment,
   Though beneath the frowns of fate,
Knaves and beggars find contentment,
   Fears and cares attend the great.

Though our creditors are fpiteful,
   And reftrain our bodies here,
Ufe will make a jail delightful,
   Since there's nothing elfe to fear.
Every ifland's but a prifon,
   Strongly guarded by the fea:
Kings and princes, for that reafon,
   Pris'ners are as well as we.

What was it made great Alexander,
   Weep at his unfriendly fate?
'Twas becaufe he could not wander
   Beyond the world's ftrong prifon-gate.
The world itfelf is ftrongly bounded
   By the heavens and ftars above:
Why fhould we then be confounded,
   Since there's nothing free but love?

SONG LXV.

MY TEMPLES WITH CLUSTERS.

Yet why this refolve to relinquifh the fair?
'Tis a folly with fpirits like mine to defpair;
For what mighty charms can be found in a glafs,
If not fill'd to the health of fome favourite lafs?

'Tis woman whofe charms every rapture impart,
And lend a new fpring to the pulfe of the heart;
The mifer himfelf, fo fupreme is her fway,
Grows a convert to love, and refigns her the key.

At the found of her voice forrow lifts up her head,
And poverty liftens, well pleas'd, from her fhed;
While age, in an ecftacy, hob'ling along,
Beats time, with his crutch, to the tune of her fong.

Then bring me a goblet from Bacchus's hoard,
The largeft and deepeft that ftands on his board;
I'll fill up a brimmer, and drink to the fair;
'Tis the thirft of a lover—and pledge me who dare!

SONG LXVI.
LOW DOWN IN THE BROOM.

My daddy is a canker'd carle, He'll nae twin wi' his gear, My minny she's a scolding wife, hads a' the house asteer. But let them say, or let them do, it's a' ane to me; For he's low down he's in the broom, that's waiting on me, waiting on me, my love, he's waiting on me, For he's low down he's in the broom, That's waiting for me.

My aunty Kate fits at her wheel,
 And fair fhe lightlies me ;
But weel ken I it's a' envy ;
 For ne'er a jo has fhe.
But let them fay, &c.

My coufin Kate was fair beguil'd
 Wi' Johnnie i' the glen :
And aye fince fyne, fhe cries, beware
 Of falfe deluding men.
But let her fay, &c.

Glee'd Sandy he came weft ae night,
 And fpeer'd when I faw Pate,
And aye fince fyne the neighbours round
 They jeer me air and late.

But let them fay, or let them do,
 It's a' ane to me ;
For I'll gae to the bonny lad
 That's waiting on me ;
Waiting on me, my love,
 He's waiting on me ;
For he's low down, he's in the broom
 That's waiting for me.

SONG LXVII.

HOW LITTLE DO THE LANDMEN KNOW.

How little do the landmen know, of what we sai-

lors feel, When waves do mount, and winds do blow,

but we have hearts of steel.   No danger can

a-fright us, no enemy shall flout, we'll make the

monsieurs right us, so toss the cann about.

Sick stout to orders messmates,
  We'll plunder, burn, and sink,
Then France have at your first rates,
  For Britons never shrink.
We'll rummage all we fancy,
  We'll bring them in by scores,
And Moll and Kate and Nancy,
  Shall roll in louis d'ors.

L iij

While here at Deal we're ly'ng,
  With our noble commodore,
We'll spend our wages freely boys,
  And then to sea for more.
In peace we'll drink and sing boys,
  In war we'll never fly,
Here's a health to George our king, boys,
  And the royal family.

SONG LXVIII.

WHRE'S MY SWAIN.

Where's my swain so blithe and clever, why d'ye

leave me all in sorrow? Three whole days are gone

for ever, since you said you'd come to - morrow,

If you lov'd but half as I do, you'd been here with

looks so bonny, Love has fly-ing wings I well

know, not for ling'ring la - - zy Johnny, Love

has flying wings I well know, not for ling'ring

la - zy Johnny.

What can he be now a doing,
  Is he with the lasses Maying?
He had better here be wooing,
  Than with others fondly playing.
Tell me truly where he's roving,
  That I may no longer sorrow;
If he's weary grown of loving,
  Let him tell me so to-morrow.

Does some fav'rite rival hide thee,
  Let her be the happy creature,
I'll not plague myself to chide thee,
  Nor dispute with her a feature.
But I can't and will not tarry,
  Nor will kill myself with sorrow,
I may loose the time to marry,
  If I wait beyond to-morrow.

Think not shepherd thus to brave me,
  If I'm your's pray wait no longer,
If you won't another 'll have me,
  I may cool but not grow fonder.

If your lovers, girls, forsake ye,
　Whine not in despair and sorrow,
Blest another lad may make ye;
　Stay for none beyond to-morrow.

SONG LXIX.
VARIETY IS CHARMING.
Tune—*You the point may carry*—Page 118.

I'M in love with twenty,
　I'm love with twenty,
　　And could adore
　　As many more,
There's nothing like a plenty.

　Variety is charming,
　Variety is charming,
　　A constancy
　　Is not for me,
　So ladies take your warning.

For a man in one love,
For a man in one love,
　　He looks as poor
　　As any boor,
For a man in one love.
　Variety, &c.

Girls grown old and ugly,
Girls grown old and ugly,
　　They can't inspire
　　The same desire,
As when they're young and smugly.
　Variety, &c.

'Tis not the grand **regalia**,
'Tis not the grand regalia
　　Of eastern kings
　　That poets sings,
But O the sweet seraglio.
　Variety, &c.

SONG LXX.
AS SURE AS A GUN.

Says Co-lin to me, I've a thought in my head,
I know a young damsel I'm dying to wed, I
know a young damsel I'm dying to wed. So
please you, quoth I, and whene'er it is done, you'll
quarrel and you'll part again, as sure as a gun! As
sure as a gun! As sure as a gun! You'll quarrel
and you'll part again as sure as a gun.

And so when you're married (poor amorous wight!
You'll bill it, and coo it from morning till night:
But trust me, good Colin, you'll find it bad fun,—
Instead of which you'll fight and scratch—as sure as a gun!

But shou'd she prove fond of her own dearest love,
And you be as supple, and soft as her glove;
Yet be she a saint, and as chaste as a nun—
You're fasten'd to her apron-strings—as sure as a gun!

Suppose it was you then, said he, with a leer;
You wou'd not serve me so, I'm certain, my dear:
In troth I replied, I will answer for none,—
But do as other women do—as sure as a gun!

SONG LXXI.

FAL DE RAL TIT.

'Twas I learnt a pretty song in France, And I

brought it o'er the sea by chance; And then in Wapping

I did dance, Oh! the like was never seen: For I

made the music loud for to play, All for to pass the

dull hours a-way, And when I had nothing left for

to say, Then I sung Fal de ral tit, Tit fal de ral,

Chorus.

Tit fal de ray, Then I sung Fal de ral tit, Then we

sung Fal de ral tit.

As I was walking down Thames street,
A ship mate of mine I chanc'd for to meet,
And I was resolv'd him for to treat,
With a cann of grog, gillio!
A cann of grog they brought us strait,
All for to pleasure my ship mate,
And satisfaction give him strait,
Then I sung Fal de ral tit, &c.

The macaronies next came in,
All drest so neat, and look'd so trim,
And thinking for to strike me dum.
There was half a score or more.
Some was short, and some was tall,
But 'tis very well known that I lick'd them all,
For I dous'd their heads against the wall,
    Then I sung Fal de ral tit, &c.

The landlord then aloud did fay,
As how he wifh'd I wou'd go away;
And if I 'tempted for to ftay,
As how he'd take the law,
Lord d—me, fays I, you may do your worft,
For I've not fcarcely quench'd my thirft,
All this I faid, and nothing worfe,
Then I fung Fal de ral tit, &c.

It's when I've croft the raging main,
And be come back to Old England again,
Of grog I'll drink galore;
With a pretty girl for to fit by my fide,
And for her coftly robes I'll provide,
So that fhe fhall be fatisfied,
Then I'll fing Fal de ral tit, &c.

SONG LXXII.
ANDRO WI' HIS CUTTY GUN.

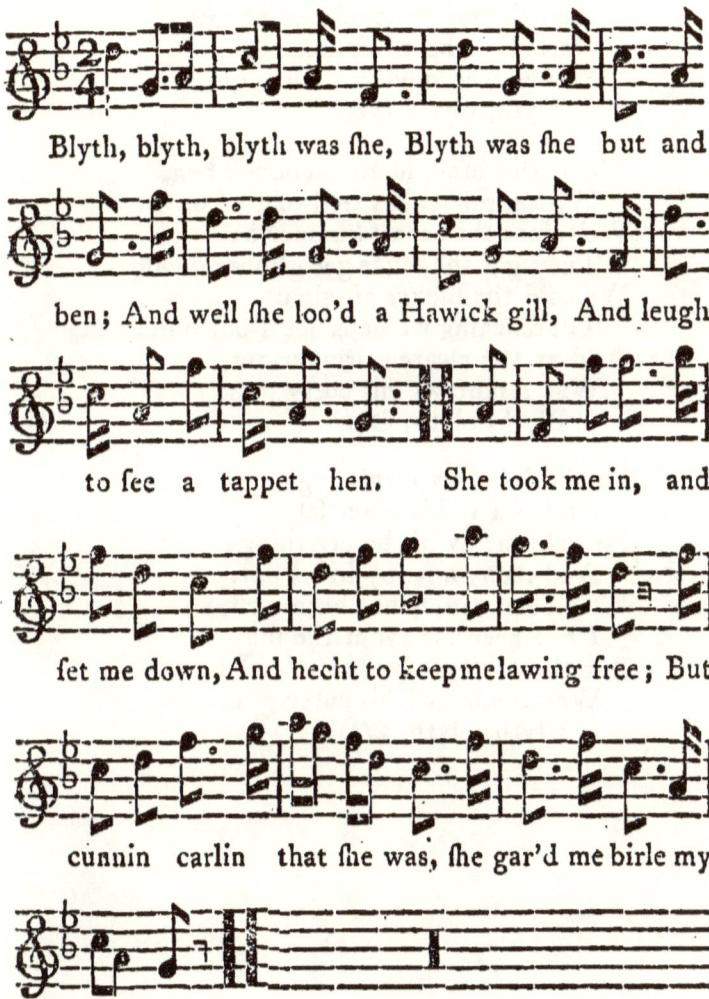

Blyth, blyth, blyth was she, Blyth was she but and ben; And well she loo'd a Hawick gill, And leugh to see a tappet hen. She took me in, and set me down, And hecht to keep me lawing free; But cunnin carlin that she was, she gar'd me birle my bawbee.

We loo'd the liquor well enough;
　But waes my heart my cafh was done,
Before that I had quench'd my drouth,
　And laith I was to pawn my fhoon.
When we had three times toom'd our ftoup,
　And the neift chappin new begun,
In ftarted, to heeze up our hope,
　Young Andro wi' his cutty gun.
　　Blyth, blyth, &c.

The carlin brought her kebbuck ben,
　With girdle-cakes well toafted brown;
Well does the canny kimmer ken,
　They gar the fcuds gae glibber down.
We ca'd the bicker aft about,
　Till dawning we ne'er jee'd our bum.
And ay the cleareft drinker out,
　Was Andro wi' his cutty gun.
　　Blyth, blyth, &c.

He did like ony mavis fing,
　And as I in his oxter fat,
He ca'd me ay his bonny thing,
　And mony a fappy kifs I gat.
I hae been eaft, I hae been weft,
　I hae been far ayont the fun;
But the blytheft lad that e'er I faw,
　Was Andro wi' his cutty gun.
　　Blyth, blyth, &c.

SONG LXXIII.
BIRKS OF INVERMAY.

The smiling morn, the breathing spring, invite the tuneful birds to sing, And while they warble from each spray, love melts the u-ni-ver-sal lay. Let us, A-man-da, timely wise, like them im-prove the hour that flies, and in soft raptures waste the day, A-mong the birks of In-ver-may.

For soon the winter of the year,
And age, life's winter, will appear;
At this thy living bloom will fade,
As that will strip the verdant shade;
Our taste of pleasure then is o'er,
The feather'd songsters are no more;
And when they droop, and we decay,
Adieu the birks of Invermay.

Behold the hills and vales around,
With lowing herds and flocks abound;
The wanton kids, and frisking lambs,
Gambol and dance about their dams;
The busy bees with humming noise,
And all the reptile kind rejoice;
Let us, like them, then sing and play
About the birks of Invermay.

Hark, how the waters, as they fall,
Loudly my love to gladness call;
The wanton waves sport in the beams,
And fishes play throughout the streams;
The circling sun does now advance,
And all the planets round him dance:
Let us as jovial be as they
Among the birks of Invermay.

MISCELLANY. 137

SONG LXXIV.

FRIEND AND PITCHER.

Moderato.

The wealthy fool, with gold in store, will still desire to grow richer, give me but these, I ask no more, My charming girl, my friend, and pitcher. Chorus. My friend so rare, my girl so fair, With such, what mortal can be richer; Give me but these, a fig for care, With my sweet girl, my friend, and pitcher.

M iij

From morning fun I'd never grieve
  To toil a hedger or a ditcher,
If that, when I come home at eve,
  I might enjoy my friend and pitcher.
    My friend fo rare, &c.

Tho' fortune ever fhuns my door,
  I know not what can bewitch her;
With all my heart can I be poor,
  With my fweet girl, my friend, and pitcher.
    My friend fo rare, &c.

SONG LXXV.
THO' LATE I WAS PLUMP.

Tho' late I was plump, round, and jolly, I now am as thin as a rod, Oh love is the caufe of my folly, and foon I'll lie under a fod. Sing ditherum doodle, nagety, nagety, tragety, rum, and goofe- therum foodle, Fidgety, fidgety, nigety, mum.

Dear Kathleen, then why did you flout me,
   A lad that's fo cofey and warm.
Oh! ev'ry thing's handfome about me,
   My cabin and fnug little farm.
      Sing ditherum, &c.

What tho' I have fcrap'd up no money,
   No duns at my chamber attend;

On Sunday I ride on my poney.
And still have a bit for a friend.
  Sing ditherum, &c.

The cock courts his hens all around me,
  The sparrow, the pigeon, and dove;
Oh! how all this courting confounds me,
  When I look and think of my love.
    Sing ditherum, &c.

SONG LXXVI.
NOW PHŒBUS GILDS.

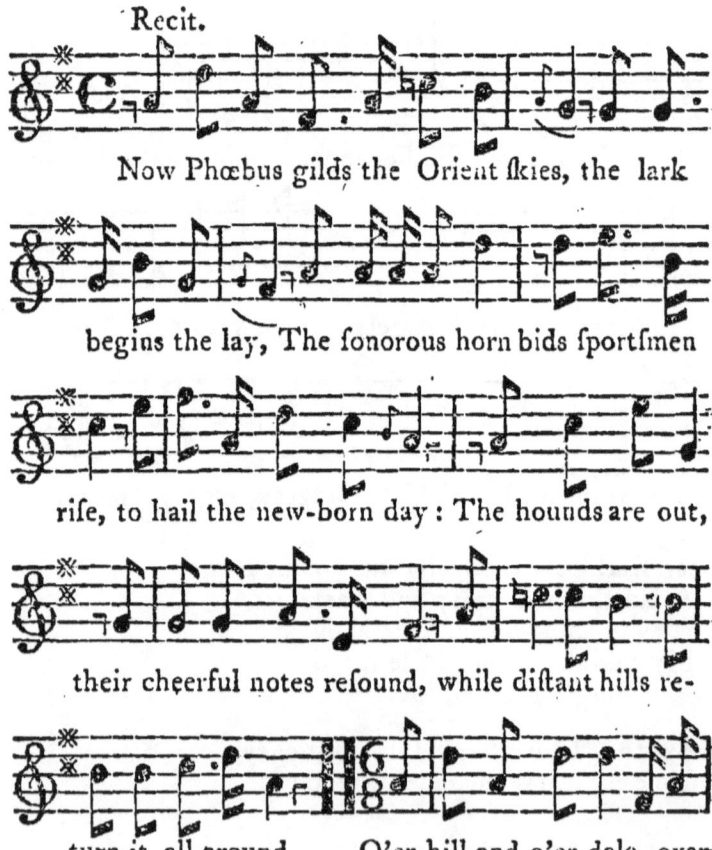

Now Phœbus gilds the Orient skies, the lark begins the lay, The sonorous horn bids sportsmen rise, to hail the new-born day: The hounds are out, their cheerful notes resound, while distant hills re-turn it all around. O'er hill and o'er dale, over

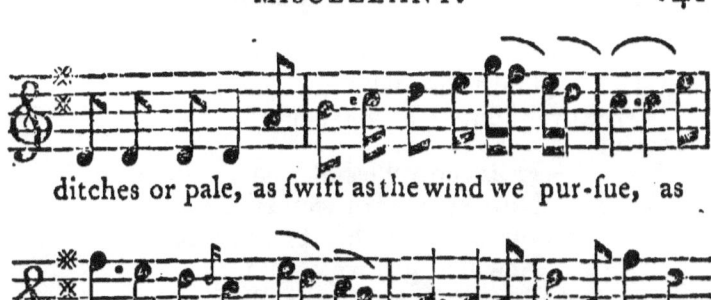

ditches or pale, as swift as the wind we pur-sue, as

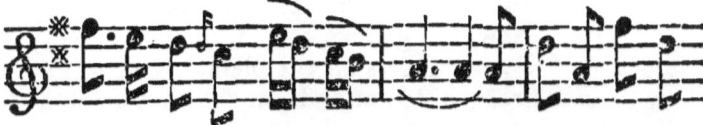

swift as the wind we pur - - sue, the fox or the hare,

or the swift footed deer, no matter what sport is in

view -

- - - No matter what sport is in view.

 Health waits on the chace,
 Paints with blushes the face,
Spleen and vapours are left in the rear
  The brooks and the floods,
  And the deep embrown'd woods,
Delightful around us appear.

  To the sports of the field
  All others must yield,
For hunting's of ancient renown ;

Kings and princes, of old,
Have this paftime extoll'd,
Royal hunters have fat on the throne.

Hills and vallies o'erpaft,
Now homeward we hafte,
And our miftreffes hearty embrace:
New ftrength we obtain,
By our fports on the plain,
For ftrength ftill attends on the chace.

Now the bowl comes in view,
Which with glee we purfue,
And thus happily finifh the day:
To the huntrefs divine,
To Diana we join,
While each chorus loudly huzza.

SONG LXXVII.

HOOLY AND FAIRLY.

Oh! what had I a-do for to marry; My wife she

drinks naething but sack and canary, I to her friends

complain'd right airly: O gin my wife wou'd drink

hooly and fairly, Hooly and fairly, Hooly and fairly;

O gin my wife wou'd drink hooly and fairly.

First she drank Crummie, and syne she drank Garie,
Now she has drunken my bonny gray marie,
That carried me thro' the dub and the larie.
    Oh! gin my wife, &c.

If she'd drink but her ain things, I wad na much care,
She drinks my claiths I canna well spare,
To the kirk and the market I gang fu' barely.
    Oh! gin my wife, &c.

If there's ony filler, fhe maun keep the purfe;
If I feek but a baubee, fhe'll fcald and fhe'll curfe;
She gangs like a queen, I fcrimpet and fparely.
    Oh! gin my wife, &c.

I never was given to wrangling nor ftrife,
Nor e'er did refufe her the comforts of life,
E'er it come to a war, I am ay for a parley.
    Oh! gin my wife, &c.

A pint wi' her cummers I wad her allow,
But when fhe fits down fhe fills herfel fou;
And when fhe is fou, fhe's unco' camfterie.
    Oh! gin my wife, &c.

She rins out to the cafey, fhe roars and fhe rants,
Has nae dread o' her nibours, nor minds the houfe wants,
But fings fome fool-fang, Tak' up your heart Charlie.
    Oh! gin my wife, &c.

And when fhe comes hame fhe lays on the lads,
She ca's the laffes baith limmers and jades,
And I my ainfel an auld cuckold carlie,
    Oh! gin my wife, &c.

SONG LXXVIII.

GOOD MORROW TO YOUR NIGHT-CAP.

Dear Kathleen you no doubt find Sleep how very

sweet 'tis, Dogs bark, and cocks have crow'd out you ne-

ver dream how late 'tis. This morning gay, I

post away, to have with you a bit of play, on two legs

rid a-long to bid, good morrow to your night cap.

Last night a little browsy,
  With whisky, ale, and cyder,
I ask'd young Betty Blousy
  To let me sit beside her;
    Her anger rose,
    And sour as sloes,
  The little gipsey cock'd her nose.
Yet here I've rid along to bid,
  Good-morrow to your night-cap.

N

SONG LXXIX.

HOW STANDS THE GLASS AROUND.

MISCELLANY.

bound. The trumpets sound, the colours
bound. The trumpets sound, the colours
they are flying, boys, to fight, kill, or wound, may
they are flying, boys, to fight, kill, or wound, may
we still be found, con-tent with our hard
we still be found, con-tent with our hard
fate, my boys, on the cold ground.
fate, my boys, on the cold ground.

Why, foldiers, why,
Shou'd we be melancholy, boys?
Why, foldiers, why?
Whofe bufinefs 'tis to die!
What, fighing? fie!
Don't fear, drink on, be jolly, boys!
'Tis he, you, or I!
Cold, hot, wet, or dry,
We're always bound to follow, boys,
And fcorn to fly!

'Tis but in vain,—
I mean not to upbraid you, boys,—
'Tis but in vain
For foldiers to complain,
Should next campaign
Send us to him who made us, boys,
We're free from pain!
But, if we remain,
A bottle and kind landlady
Cure all again.

SONG LXXX.
THE CONTENTED MAN.

The man that's contented is void of all care,

Tol de rol tol de rol tol de rol la dy, He far o-

ver tops the foul flave-ry of fear, Tol de rol tol

de rol tol de rol la dy. A mind that's ferene, and

a body in health, gives a man all the pleafure

and grandeur of wealth. Tol de rol la dy, Tol de

rol la dy, Tol de rol tol de rol tol de rol la dy.

Laſt day I went out with a heart full of joy,
  Tol de rol, &c.
Which nothing but vice or ſharp pain could annoy;
  Tol de rol, &c.
The firſt that I met was a miſer, whoſe gloom
Shew'd a ſoul that was muddy, and ſtraiten'd in room.
  Tol de rol, &c.

In Britain's fair iſland there's none to be ſeen
  Tol de rol, &c.
Of more ſullen, ſelfiſh, and ſordid a mein;
  Tol de rol, &c.
Regardleſs of honour, a ſlave to his gold,
Deſpis'd of the young, and contemn'd of the old,
  Tol de rol, &c.

The next that I met was a profligate aſs,
  Tol de rol, &c.
Whoſe brains were of cork, and his forehead of braſs;
  Tol de rol, &c.
By game he was galloping thro' his eſtate,
And mis'ry attended his ſad ſinking fate.

O place me, kind heav'n! in what ſtation you pleaſe,
  Tol de rol, &c.
So my body's in health, and my ſoul be at eaſe;
  Tol de rol, &c.
By command of myſelf, independent and free,
Contentment ſhall ſtill be a pleaſure to me.
  Tol de rol, &c.

O rather in a cottage may I be fed
  Tol de rol, &c.
With roots the moſt common, and coarſeſt brown bread,
  Tol de rol, &c.
Than to riot with luxury, fopp'ry, and vice,
They're the loſs of contentment, too precious a prize.
  Tol de rol, &c.

Let rakes ramble after their harlots and wine,
 Tol de rol, &c.
'Till with poxes and palsies their carcases dwine ;
 Tol de rol, &c.
Grow old while they're young, and have wasted their store,
While the vot'ries of Virtue are blithe at fourscore.
 Tol de rol, &c.

The thunder may roar, and the hurricanes make
 Tol de rol, &c.
The ocean to boil, and the forests to shake ;
 Tol de rol, &c.
The light'ning may flash, and the rocks may be rent,
But nothing can ruffle the mind that's content.

This world's well freighted with wonders in store,
 Tol de rol, &c.
And we're sent into it to think and explore ;
 Tol de rol, &c.
And when the due summons shall call us away,
No more's to be said, but contented obey.
 Tol de rol, &c.

SONG LXXXI.
THE LAND OF DELIGHT.

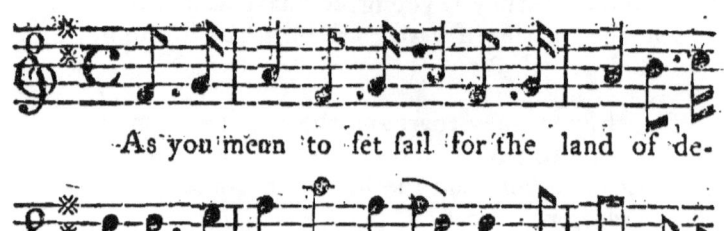

As you mean to set sail for the land of de-

light, And in wedlock's soft hammock to swing ev'ry

night; If you hope that your voyage suc-cefs-ful

shou'd prove, Fill your sails with affection, your ca-

bins with love. If you hope that your voyage

successful shou'd prove, fill your sails with affec-

tion, your cabins with love. Fill your sails with

affection, your ca - bins with love.

Let your heart, like the main-maſt, be ever upright,
And the union you boaſt, like our takle, be tight;
Of the ſhoals of indiff'rence be ſure to keep clear,
And the quickſands of jealouſy never come near.

But if vapours and whims, like ſea-ſickneſs, prevail,
You muſt ſpread all your canvas, and catch the freſh gale,
For, if briſk blows the wind, and there comes a rough
    ſea,
You muſt lower your top-ſail, and ſcud under lee.

If huſbands e'er hope to live peaceable lives,
They muſt reckon themſelves, give the helm to their
    wives;
For the ſmoother we ſail, boys, we're ſafeſt from harm,
And on ſhipboard the head is ſtill rul'd by the helm.

Then liſt to your pilot, my boys, and be wiſe;
If my precepts you ſcorn, and my maxims deſpiſe,
A brace of proud antlers your brows may adorn,
And a hundred to one, but you double Cape Horn.

SONG LXXXII.
THE LITTLE MAN AND MAID.

There was a little man, and he woo'd a little

maid, And he said, little maid, will you wed, wed wed.

I have little more to say, than will you, aye or

nay, For little said is soon - eft mended-ed.

The little maid reply'd, Little Sir, you've little said,
  To induce a little maiden to wed;
You muſt ſay a little more, and produce a little ſtore,
  'Ere I to the church will be led.

The little man reply'd, If you'll be my little bride,
  I will raiſe my little note a little higher:
Tho' I've little for to prate, yet my little heart is great,
  By the little god of love I'm on fire.

The little maid reply'd, If I be your little bride,
  Pray, what would you give me to eat?
Would the flame that you're so rich in, put a fire into
    the kitchen,
  Or the little god of love stir the spit?

The little man reply'd, and some say a little cry'd,
  For his little heart was fill'd with sorrow,
With the little that I have I will be your little slave,
  And the rest, my little dear, we will borrow.

Thus did the little gent. make the little maid relent,
  For her little heart began for to beat;
Tho' his offers were but small, she accepted of them all,
  Now she thanks her little stars for her fate.

SONG LXXXIII.
DONNEL AND FLORA.

When merry hearts were gay, Carelefs of ought

but play, Poor Flo-ra flipt away, fad'ning to Mo-

ra, Loofe flow'd her coal black hair, quick heav'd

her bofom bare, And thus to the troubled air

fhe vented her for-row.

" Loud howls the northern blaft,
" Bleak is the dreary wafte ;—
" Hafte, then, O Donnel, hafte,
   " Hafte to thy Flora.
" Twice twelve long months are o'er,
" Since in a foreign fhore,
" You promis'd to fight no more,
   " But meet me in Mora.

" Where now is Donnel dear?
" Maids cry with taunting sneer,
" Say, is he still sincere
        " To his lov'd Flora.
" Parents upbraid my moan;
" Each heart is turn'd to stone—
" Ah Flora! thou'rt now alone,
    " Friendless in Mora.

" Come then, O come away,
" Donnel no longer stay;
" Where can my rover stray
        " From his dear Flora.
" Ah sure he ne'er could be
" False to his vows and me.
" O heav'n, is not yonder he
        " Bounding in Mora."

" Never, O wretched fair,"
(Sigh'd the sad messenger)
" Never shall Donnel mair
        " Meet his lov'd Flora.
" Cold, cold beyond the main
" Donnel thy love lies slain;
" He sent me to soothe thy pain
    " Weeping in Mora.

" Well fought our gallant men,
" Headed by brave Burgoyne;
" Our heroes were thrice led on
        " To British glory.
" But ah! tho' our foes did flee,
" Sad was the loss to thee,
" While ev'ry fresh victory
        " Drown'd us in sorrow."

" Here, take this trusty blade,"
(Donnel expiring said)
" Give it to yon dear maid
    " Weeping in Mora;
            O

" Tell her, O Allan tell,
" Donnel thus bravely fell,
" And that in his laſt farewell,
   " He thought on his Flora."

Mute ſtood the trembling fair,
Speechleſs with wild deſpair,
Then ſtriking her boſom bare,
   Sigh'd out poor Flora,
" Oh Donnel! O welladay!"
Was all the fond heart could ſay :
At length the ſound died away,
   Feebly in Mora.

SONG LXXXIV.
MY JO JANET.

O sweet Sir, for your courtesie, When you come

by the Bass, then, And for the love ye bear to me,

buy me a keeking glass, then. Keek into the

draw-well, Janet, Janet, And there ye'll see your

bonny sell, My jo Janet.

Keeking in the draw-well clear,
   What if I shou'd fa' in, Sir?
Syne a' my kin will say and swear,
   I drown'd mysel for sin, Sir.
Had the better be the brae,
      Janet, Janet;
Had the better be the brae,
      My jo Janet.

O ij

Good Sir, for your courtefie,
  Coming through Aberdeen, then,
For the love ye bear to me,
  Buy me a pair of fheen, then.
Clout the auld, the new are dear,
      Janet, Janet;
Ae pair may gain ye ha'f a year,
      My jo Janet.

But what if dancing on the green,
  And fkipping like a mawkin,
If they fhould fee my clouted fheen,
  O' me they will ke taukin.
Dance ay laigh, and late at e'en,
      Janet, Janet,
Syne a' their fauts will no be feen,
      My jo Janet.

Kind Sir, for your courtefie,
  When ye gae to the crofs, then,
For the love ye bear to me,
  Buy me a pacing horfe, then.
Pace upo' your fpinning wheel,
      Janet, Janet;
Pace upo' your fpinning wheel,
      My jo Janet.

My fpinning wheel is auld and ftiff,
  The rock o't winna ftand, Sir,
To keep the temper-pin in tiff,
  Employs aft my hand, Sir.
Make the beft o't that ye can,
      Janet, Janet,
But like it never wale a man,
      My-jo Janet.

SONG LXXXV.
O GREEDY MIDAS.

O greedy Midas, I've been told, that what you touch you turn to gold, that what you touch you turn to gold. O had I but a pow'r like thine, O had I but a pow'r like thine, I'd turn, I'd turn whate'er I touch to wine. I'd turn whate'er I touch to wine.

O iij

Each purling stream shou'd feel my force,
Each fish my fatal power mourn,
    Each fish, &c.
And wond'ring at the mighty change,
    And wond'ring, &c.
Shou'd in their native regions burn,
    Shou'd in, &c.

Nor shou'd there any dare t' approach
Unto my mantling sparkling shrine,
    Unto my, &c.
But first shou'd pay their votes to me,
    But first, &c.
And stile me only god of wine.
    And style, &c.

SONG LXXVIII.
TWINE WEEL THE PLAIDEN.

O I hae loſt my ſilken ſnood, that tied my hair ſo yellow, I've gi'en my heart to the lad I lood, he was a gal-lant fel-low. And twine it weel my bonny dow, and twine it weel the plaiden, the laſſie loſt her ſilken ſnood, in pu'ing of the bracken.

He prais'd my e'en fae bonny blue,
  Sae lilly white my fkin, O,
And fyne he prie'd my bonny mou',
  And fwore it was nae fin, O.
And twine it weel, my bonny dow,
  And twine it weel the plaiden;
The laffie loft her filken fnood,
  In pu'ing of the bracken.

But he has left the lafs he lco'd,
  His ain true love forfaken,
Which gars me fair to greet the fnood,
  I loft among the bracken.
And twine it weel, my bonny dow,
  And twine it weel the plaiden;
The laffie loft her filken fnood,
  In pu'ing of the bracken.

SONG LXXXVII.

COME ROUSE BROTHER SPORTSMEN.

Come roufe brother fportfmen, the hunters all cry,

We've got a ftrong fcent, and a favouring fky, we've

got a ftrong fcent we've got a ftrong fcent we've got

Bright Phœbus has shewn us the glimpse of his face,
Peep'd in at our windows, and call'd to the chace,
He soon will be up; for his dawn wears away,
And makes the fields blush with the beams of his ray.

Sweet Molly may teaze you perhaps to lie down,
And if you refuse her perhaps she may frown,
But tell her sweet love must to hunting give place,
For as well as her charms, there are charms in the chace.

Look yonder, look yonder, old Reynard I spy,
At his brush nimbly follows brisk Chanter aud Fly,
They seize on their prey, see his eye-balls they roll,
We're in at the death, now return to the bowl.

There we'll fill up our glasses, and toast to the King,
From a bumper fresh loyalty ever will spring,
To George peace and plenty may heaven dispense;
And fox hunters flourish a thousand years hence.

SONG LXXXVIII.

THE OLD WOMAN's SONG.

Old women we are, and as wise in the chair, and

as fit for the quorum as men.   We can scold

on the bench, and ex-a-mine a wench, and like them, and like them, and like them can be wrong now and then, now and then, now and then, and like them can be wrong now and then. For look the world thro' and you'll find, nine in ten, Old wo-men can do, Old wo-men can do, Old wo-men can do, as much as old men.

We can hear a fad cafe, with a no-meaning face,
 And tho' fhallow, yet feem to be deep;
Leave all to the clerk, and when matters grow dark,
 Their worfhips had better go fleep.
  For look, &c.

When our wifdom is tafk'd, and hard queftions are afk'd,
 We anfwer them beft with a fnore;
We can mump a tit bit, and can joke without wit,
 And what can their worfhips do more.
  For look, &c.

SONG LXXXIX.
WHEN MY WIFE IS LAID IN GROUND.

O what pleasures will abound, When my wife

is laid in ground. Let earth cover her, we'll

dance over her, when my wife is laid in

ground.

Oh how happy should I be,
Wou'd little Nysa pig with me;
How I'd mumble her, touze and tumble her,
Wou'd little Nysa pig with me.

P

SONG XC.
THE HIGHLAND LADDIE.

If I were free at will to chufe
   To be the wealthieſt lawland lady,
I'd take young Donald without trews,
   With bonnet blew, and belted plaidy.
      O my bonny, &c.

The braweſt beau in burrow's-town,
   In a' his airs, with art made ready,
Compar'd to him, he's but a clown;
   He's finer far in's belted plaidy.
      O my bonny, &c.

O'er benty hills with him I'll run,
  And leave my lawland kin and daddy;
Frae winter's cauld, and summer's sun,
  He'll screen me with his Highland plaidy.
    O my bonny, &c.

A painted room, and silken bed,
  May please a lawland laird and lady;
But I can kiss, and be as glad,
  Behind a bush in's Highland plaidy.
    O my bonny, &c.

Few compliments between us pass,
  I ca' him my dear Highland laddie,
And he ca's me his lawland lass,
  Syne rows me in beneath his plaidy.
    O my bonny, &c.

Nae greater joy I'll e'er pretend,
  Than that his love prove true and steady,
Like mine to him, which ne'er shall end,
  While heaven preserves my Highland laddie.
    O my bonny, &c.

SONG XCI.
WHY HEAVES.

Why heaves my fond bo-som! Ah! what can it mean: Why flut-ters my heart which was once so se-rene. Why this sigh-ing and trembling, when Daphne is near; Or why when she's ab-sent, this sor-row and fear; Or why when she's absent, this sor-row and fear.

For ever, methinks, I with wonder could trace,
The thoufand foft charms that embellifh thy face;
Each moment I view thee, new beauties I find,
With thy face I am charm'd, but enflav'd by thy mind.

Untainted with folly, unfullied by pride,
There native good humour, and virtue refide;
Pray heaven that virtue thy foul may fupply
With compaffion for him who without thee muft die.

SONG XCII.

SINCE YOU MEAN TO HIRE.

With three crowns, your ſtanding wages,
   You ſhall daintily be fed;
Bacon, beans, ſalt-beef, and cabbage,
   Butter, milk, and oaten bread.
      Farra diddle, &c.

Come, ſtrike hands, you'll live in clover,
　When we get you once at home;
And when daily labour's over,
　We'll all dance to your ſtrum ſtrum.
　　Farra diddle, &c.

Done, ſtrike hands, I take your offer,
　Farther on I may fare worſe;
Zooks, I can no longer ſuffer
　Hungry guts and empty purſe.
　　Farra diddle, &c.

SONG CXIII.
BY THE GAILY.

By the gaily circling glafs, We can fee how minutes pafs. By the hollow cafk we're told How the waning night grows old, How the waning night grows old. Soon, too foon, the bu-fy day drives us from our fport a-way, What have we with day to do? Sons of care, 'twas made for you! Sons of care 'twas made for you!

By the filence of the owl,
  By the chirping on the thorn,
By the butts that empty roll,
  We foretel the approach of morn.
Fill, then, fill the vacant glafs,
  Let no precious moment flip;
Flout the moralizing afs,
  Joys find entrance at the lip.

SONG CXIV.

HIGHLAND MARCH.

In the garb of old Gaul, and the fire of old

Rome, From the heath cover'd mountains of Scotia

we come: On thofe mountains the Romans attempt-

ed to reign; But our anceftors fought and they

No intemperate tables our finews unbrace ;
Nor French faith nor French fopery, our country difgrace :
Still the hoarfe founding pipe breaths the true martial ftrain,
And our hearts ftill the true Scottifh valour retain.
'Twas with anguifh and woe, that, of late, we beheld
Rebel forces rufh down from the hills to the field ;

For our hearts are devoted to George and the laws ;
And we'll fight, like true Britons, in liberty's caufe.

But ftill, at a diftance from Briton's lov'd fhore,
May her foes, in confufion, her mercy implore !
May her coafts ne'er with foreign invafions be fpread,
Nor detefted rebellion again raife it's head !
May the fury of party and faction long ceafe !
May our councils be wife, and our commerce increafe !
And, in Scotia's cold climate, may each of us find,
That our friends ftill prove true, and our beauties prove kind.

SONG XCV.

To the foregoing Tune.

IN the garb of old Gaul, wi' the fire of old Rome,
From the heath-cover'd mountains of Scotia we come,
Where the Romans endeavour'd our country to gain,
But our anceftors fought, and they fought not in vain.
  Such our love of liberty, our country, and our laws,
  That, like our anceftors of old, we ftand by freedom's caufe ;
  We'll bravely fight, like heroes bold, for honour and applaufe,
  And defy the French, with all their art, to alter our laws.

No effeminate cuftoms our finews unbrace,
No luxurious tables enervate our race;
Our loud-founding pipe bears the true martial ftrain,
So do we the old Scottifh valour retain.
  Such our love, &c.

We're tall as the oak on the mount of the vale,
Are fwift as the roe which the hind doth affail :
As the full moon in autumn our fhields do appear,
Minerva would dread to encounter our fpear.
  Such our love, &c.

As a ſtorm in the ocean when Boreas blows,
So are we enrag'd when we ruſh on our foes ;
We ſons of the mountains, tremendous as rocks,
Daſh the force of our foes with our thundering ſtrokes.
  Such our love, &c.

Quebec and Cape Breton, the pride of old France,
In their troops fondly boaſted, till we did advance ;
But when our claymores they ſaw us produce,
Their courage did fail, and they ſu'd for a truce.
  Such our love, &c.

In our realm may the fury of faction long ceaſe,
May our councils be wiſe, and our commerce increaſe,
And in Scotia's cold climate may each of us find,
That our friends ſtill prove true, and our beauties prove kind ;
Then we'll defend our liberty, our country, and our laws,
And teach our late poſterity to fight in freedom's cauſe,
That they, like our anceſtors bold, for honour and applauſe,
May defy the French and Spaniards to alter our laws.

Q

SONG CXVI.
CORN-RIGS.

My Pa-tie is a lo - - ver gay, His mind

is ne - ver mud-dy, His breath is sweeter

than new hay, His face is fair and rud-

dy. His shape is handsome, middle

Last night I met him on a bawk,
    Where yellow corn was growing,
There mony a kindly word he spake,
    That set my heart a glowing.
He kifs'd, and vow'd he wad be mine,
    And loo'd me beſt of ony;
That gars me like to ſing ſinſyne,
    O corn-rigs are bonny!

Let maidens of a filly mind
　Refuse what maist they're wanting,
Since we for yielding were defign'd,
　We chastely should be granting:
Then I'll comply, and marry Pate,
　And fyne my cockernony
He's free to touzle, air or late,
　Where corn-rigs are bonny.

SONG XCVII.

To the foregoing Tune.

LORD, what care I for mam or dad?
　Why let them scold and bellow;
For while I live I'll love my lad,
　He's such a charming fellow.
The last fair day, on yonder green,
　The youth he danc'd so well, O,
So spruce a lad was never seen,
　As my sweet charming fellow.

The fair was over, night was come,
　The lad was somewhat mellow;
Says he, my dear. I'll see you home,
　I thank'd the charming fellow.
You rogue, says I, you've stopp'd my breath,
　Ye bells ring out my knell, O,
Again I'd die so sweet a death,
　With such a charming fellow.

We trudg'd along, the moon shone bright,
　Says he, my sweetest Nell, O,
I'll kifs you here by this good light,
　Lord, what a charming fellow!
You rogue, says I, you've stopp'd my breath,
　Ye bells ring out my knell, O;
Again I'd die so sweet a death,
　With such a charming fellow.

SONG XCVIII.
SWEET ANNIE.

Sweet Annie frae the sea-beach came, Where Jocky speel'd the ves-sel's side, Ah! wha can keep their heart at hame, When Jocky's tost a-boon the tide. Far aff to di-stant realms he gangs, Yet I'll prove true as he has been; And when ilk lass a-bout him thrangs, He'll think on Annie, his faith-ful ane.

I met our wealthy laird yeſtreen,
  Wi' gou'd in hand he tempted me,
He prais'd my brow, my rolling een,
  And made a brag of what he'd gi'e:
What tho' my Jocky's far away,
  Toſt up and down the anſome main,
I'll keep my heart anither day,
  Since Jockey may return again.

Nae mair, falſe Jamie, ſing nae mair,
  And fairly caſt your pipe away;
My Jocky wad be troubled ſair,
  To ſee his friend his love betray:
For a' your ſongs and verſe are vain,
  While Jocky's notes do faithful flow;
My heart to him ſhall true remain,
  I'll keep it for my conſtant jo.

Blaw ſaft, ye gales, round Jocky's head,
  And gar your waves be calm and ſtill;
His hameward ſail with breezes ſpeed,
  And dinna a' my pleaſure ſpill.
What tho' my Jocky's far away,
  Yet he will braw in filler ſhine;
I'll keep my heart anither day,
  Since Jocky may again be mine.

MISCELLANY. 187

SONG CXIX.
WINTER.

A - dieu, ye groves, adieu, ye plains, all nature mourning lies. See gloomy clouds and thickning rains ob-fcure the lab'ring fkies. See, fee, from a-far, th' impending ftorm, with fullen hafte ap-pear, See winter comes, a dreary form, to rule the falling year.

No more the lambs with gamesome bound,
  Rejoice the gladen'd sight;
No more the gay enamell'd ground,
  Or Sylvan scenes delight.
Thus lovely Nancy, much lov'd maid;
  Thy early charms must fail,
Thy rose must droop the lilly fade,
  And winter soon prevail.

Again the lark, sweet bird of day,
  May rise on active wing,
Again the sportive herds may play,
  And hail reviving spring.
But youth, my fair, sees no return,
  The pleasing bubble's o'er,
In vain it's fleeting joys you mourn,
  They fall to bloom no more.

Haste, then, dear girl, the time improve,
  Which art can ne'er regain,
In blisful scenes of mutual love,
  With some distinguish'd swain,
So shall life's spring, like jocund May,
  Pass smiling and serene,
Thus summer, autumn, glide away,
  And winter soon prevail.

SONG C.
A POX OF YOUR POTHER.

A pox of your pother about this or that, your

shrieking or sqeaking a sharp or a flat, I'm sharp

by my bumpers, you're flat master Pol, so here goes a

set to a Tol de rol lol de rol tol de rol de

rol, tol de rol lol, tol rol tol de rol lol de rol

tol de rol lol.

Mankind are a medley, a chance medley race,
All ſtart in full cry to give dame Fortune chace ;
There's catch as catch can, hit or miſs, luck's all,
And luck's the beſt tune of life's Tol lol de rol, &c.

When Beauty her pack of poor lovers would hamper,
And after Miſs Will-o'-the-wiſp, the fools ſcamper ;
Ding-dong, in ſing-ſong, they the lady extol,
Pray what's all this fuſs for, but Tol lol de rol, &c.

I've done, pleaſe your worſhip, 'tis rather too long,
I only meant life is but an old ſong ;
The world's but a tragedy-comedy droll,
Where all act the ſcene of Tol lol de rol, &c.

SONG CI.
MY FOND SHEPHERDS.

My fond shepherds of late were so blest, Their fair nymphs were so hap-py and gay, That each night they went safely to rest, And they mer-rily sung thro' the day. But ah! what a scene must appear, Must the sweet rural pastime be o'er, Shall the tabor, the tabor no more strike the ear, Shall the dance on the green be no more.

Will the flocks from their paftures be led,
  Muft the herds go wild ftraying abroad,
Shall the looms be all ftopp'd in each fhed,
  And the fhips be all moor'd in each road,
Muft the arts be all fcatter'd around,
  And fhall commerce grow fick of it's tide,
Muft religion expire on the ground,
  And fhall virtue fink down by her fide.

SONG CII.
TAK YOUR AULD CLOAK ABOUT YE.

My Crummie is a useful cow,
　　And she is come of a good kyne;
Aft has she wet the bairns' mou',
　　And I am laith that she should tyne;
Get up, gudeman, it is fu' time,
　　The sun shines in the lift sae hie;
Sloth never made a gracious end,
　　Go tak' your auld cloak about ye.

My cloak was anes a good grey cloak,
　　When it was fitting for my wear;
But now it's scantly worth a groat,
　　For I have worn't this thirty year;
Let's spend the gear that we have won,
　　We little ken the day we'll die;
Then I'll be proud, since I have sworn
　　To have a new cloak about me.

In days when our King Robert rang,
　　His trews they coft but half-a-crown;
He said they were a groat o'er dear,
　　And ca'd the taylor thief and lown.
He was the king that wore a crown,
　　And thou the man of laigh degree,
'Tis pride puts a' the country down,
　　Sae take thy auld cloak about ye.

Every land has it's ain laugh,
　　Ilk kind of corn it has it's hool,
I think the warld is a' run wrang,
　　When ilka wife her man wad rule;
Do ye not see Rob, Jock, and Hab,
　　As they are girded gallantly?
While I sit hurklen in the ase,
　　I'll have a new cloak about me.

Gudeman, I wat 'tis thirty years
　　Since we did ane anither ken;
And we have had between us twa
　　Of lads and bonny lasses ten:

Now they are women grown and men,
　　I wifh and pray well may they be;
And if you prove a good hufband,
　　E'en tak' your auld cloak about ye.

Bell my wife, fhe lo'es nae ftrife;
　　But fhe wad guide me, if fhe can,
And to maintain an eafy life,
　　I aft maun yield, tho' I'm gudeman:
Nought's to be won at woman's hand,
　　Unlefs ye give her a' the plea:
Then I'll leave aff where I began,
　　And tak my auld cloak about me.

SONG CIII.
AH! CHLORIS.

Ah! Chloris, cou'd I now but fit, as unconcern'd as when your in-fant beau-ty cou'd beget no hap-pi-nefs nor pain. When I this dawning did admire, and prais'd

Your charms in harmless childhood lay,
    As metals in a mine ;
Age from no face takes more away,
    Than youth conceal'd in thine :

But as your charms infenfibly
  To their perfection prefs'd ;
So love as unperceiv'd did fly,
  And center'd in my breaft.

My paffion with your beauty grew,
  While Cupid at my heart,
Still as his mother favour'd you,
  Threw a new flaming dart.
Each gloried in their wanton part;
  To make a lover, he
Employ'd the utmoft of his art ;
  To make a beauty, fhe.

SONG CIV.

Tune—*The wealthy fool*—Page 137.

THE filver moon that fhines fo bright,
   I fwear, with reafon, is my teacher;
And if my minute-glafs runs right,
   We've time to drink another pitcher.
      'Tis not yet day, 'tis not yet day,
        Then why fhould we forfake good liquor?
      Until the fun-beams round us play,
        Let's jocund pufh about the pitcher.

They fay that I muft work all day,
   And fleep at night, to grow much richer;
But what is all the world can fay,
   Compar'd to mirth, my friend, and pitcher.
      'Tis not yet day, &c.

Tho' one may boaft a handfome wife,
   Yet ftrange vagaries may bewitch her;
Unvex'd I live a cheerful life,
   And boldly call for 'tother pitcher.
      'Tis not yet day, &c.

I dearly love a hearty man,
   (No fneaking milk-fop Jemmy Twitcher);
Who loves a lafs, and loves a glafs,
   And boldly calls for 'tother pitcher.
      'Tis not yet day, &c.

SONG CV.
YE SLUGGARDS.

Ye sluggards who murder your life-time in sleep

awake and pursue the fleet hare, From life say what

joy, say what pleasure you reap, that e'er could with

hunting compare, that e'er could with hunt - - - -

- - - - - ing compare, that e'er could with

hunting compare, that e'er could with hunting com-

pare. When Phœbus begins to enliven the morn, the

huntſman at-tend-ed by hounds, Rejoices and glows

at the ſound of the horn, whilſt woods the ſweet

echo reſound, whilſt woods the ſweet e - - - - -

- - cho reſound, whilſt woods the ſweet echo reſound

whilſt woods the ſweet echo reſound.

The courtier, the lawyer, the prieſt have a view,
  Nay ev'ry profeſſion the ſame,
But ſportſmen, ye mortals, no pleaſures purſue,
  But ſuch as accrue from the game.
While drunkards are pleas'd in the joys of the cup,
  And turn into day ev'ry night,
At the break of each morn the huntſman is up,
  And bounds o'er the lawns with delight.

Then quickly, my lads, to the foreſt repair,
  O'er hills, dales, and valleys let's fly,
For who can, ye gods, feel a moment of care,
  When each joy will another ſupply?
Thus each morning, each day, in raptures, we paſs,
  And deſire no comfort to ſhare,
But at night to refreſh with the bottle and glaſs,
  And feed on the ſpoil of the hare.

SONG CVI.
ALLY CROAKER.

There lived a man in Baleno crazy, who wanted a wife to make him uneafy, Long he had figh'd for dear Ally Croaker, And thus the gentle youth befpoke her, Will you marry me, dear Ally Croaker, will you marry me, dear Ally, Ally Croaker.

This artlefs young man, juft come from his fchoolery,
A novice in love, and all it's foolery;
Too dull for a wit, too grave for a joker,
And thus the gentle youth befpoke her,
    Will you marry, &c.

He drank with the father, he talk'd with the mother,
He rompt with the fifter, he gam'd with the brother;
He gam'd till he pawn'd his coat to the broker,
Which loft him the heart of his dear Ally Croaker,
    Oh! the fickle, fickle Ally Croaker,
    Oh! the fickle Ally, Ally Croaker.

To all ye young men who are fond of gaming,
Who are fpending your money, whilft others are faving,
Fortune's a'jilt, the de'il may choke her,
A jilt more inconftant than dear Ally Croaker,
    Oh! the inconftant Ally Croaker,
    Oh! the inconftant Ally, Ally Croaker.

MISCELLANY. 205

SONG CVII.
BIDE YE YET.

Gin I had a wee houſe, and a canty wee fire, a bonny wee wifie to praiſe and admire, a bonny wee yardie, a-ſide a wee burn, fareweel

Chorus.

to the bodies that yammer and mourn. Sae bide ye yet, and bide ye yet, ye little ken, what may betide you yet; ſome bonny wee body may be my lot, and I'll ay be canty wi' thinking o't.

S

When I gang afield, and come hame at e'en,
I'll get my wi wifie fu' neat and fu' clean,
And a bonny wee bairnie upon her knee,
That will cry Papa or Dady to me.
   And bide ye yet, &c.

And if there should happen ever to be
A diff'rence a'tween my wi wifie and me,
In hearty good humour, altho' she be teaz'd,
I'll kiss her, and clap her, until she be pleas'd.
   And bide ye yet, &c.

SONG CVIII.

WHEN LATE I WANDER'D.

When late I wander'd o'er the plain, From nymph
to nymph I strove in vain My wild desires to
rally, to rally, My wild de-sires to rally.
But now they're of themselves come home, and strange!

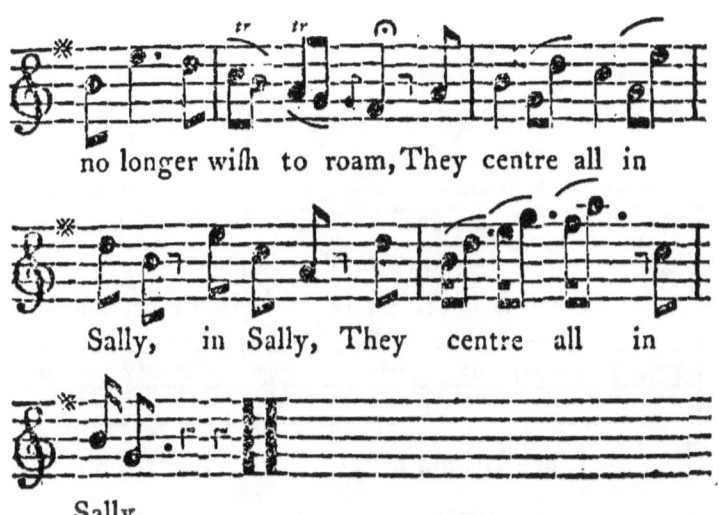

no longer wish to roam, They centre all in Sally, in Sally, They centre all in Sally.

Yet she, unkind one, damps my joy,
And cries I court but to destroy;
　　Can love with ruin tally?
By those dear lips, those eyes, I swear,
I wou'd all deaths, all torments bear,
　　Rather than injure Sally.

Come then, O come, thou sweeter far,
Than violets and roses are,
　　Or lillies of the valley;
O follow love, and quit your fear,
He'll guide you to these arms, my dear,
　　And make me blest in Sally.

SONG CIX.

RULE, BRITANNIA.

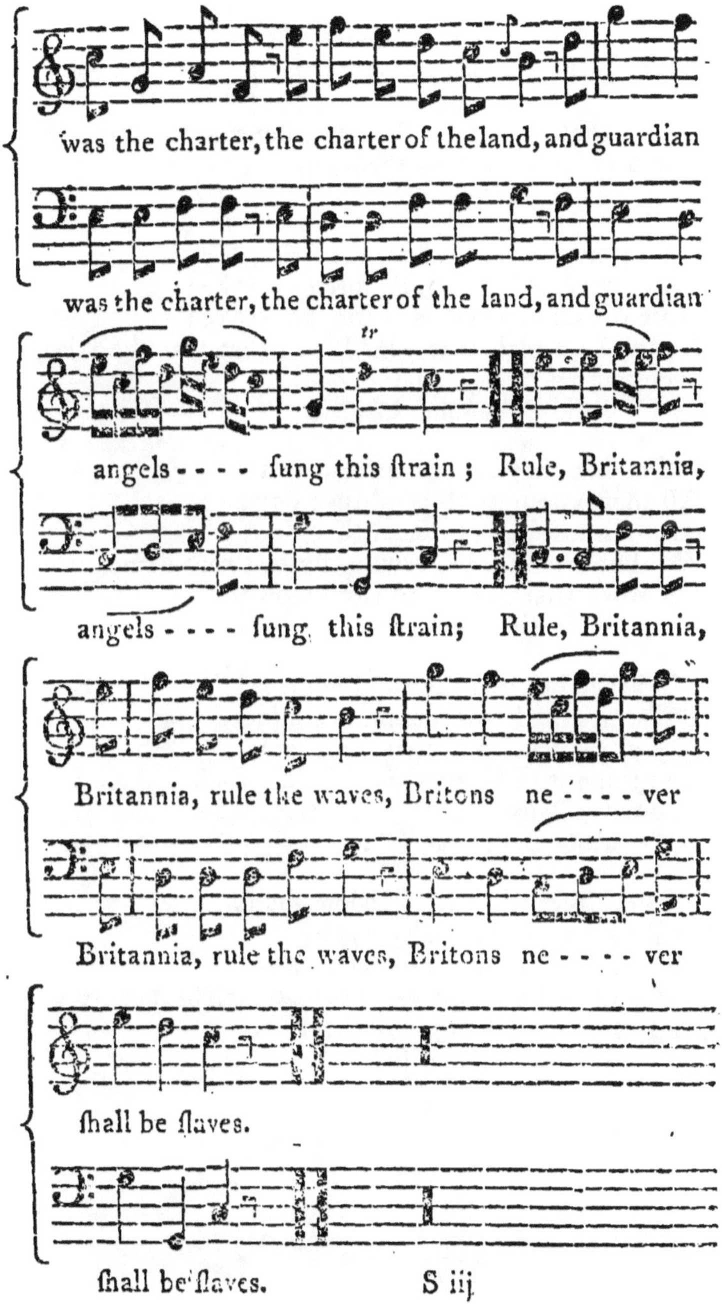

was the charter, the charter of the land, and guardian

was the charter, the charter of the land, and guardian

angels ---- sung this strain; Rule, Britannia,

angels ---- sung this strain; Rule, Britannia,

Britannia, rule the waves, Britons ne----ver

Britannia, rule the waves, Britons ne----ver

shall be slaves.

shall be slaves.

The nations, (not so blest as thee)
Must, in their turns, to tyrants fall;
Must, in their turns, to tyrants fall;
Whilst thou shalt flourish—shalt flourish great and free,
The dread and envy of them all.
  Rule Britannia, &c.

Still more majestic shalt thou rise,
More dreadful, from each foreign stroke;
More dreadful, from each foreign stroke;
As the loud blast that—loud blast that tear the skies,
Serve but to root the native oak.
  Rule Britannia, &c.

The haughty tyrants ne'er shall tame.
All their attempts to bend thee down,
All their attempts to bend thee down,
Will but arouse thy—arouse thy gen'rous flame,
But work their woe, and thy renown.
  Rule Britannia, &c.

To thee belongs the rural reign;
Thy cities shall with commerce shine,
Thy cities shall with commerce shine;
And thine shall be the—shall be the subject main;
And ev'ry shore it circles, thine.
  Rule Britannia, &c.

The Muses still with freedom found,
Shall to thy happy coasts repair,
Shall to thy happy coasts repair:
Blest isle! with matchless—with matchless beauty crown'd,
And manly hearts to guard the Fair.
  Rule Britannia, &c.

SONG CX.

To the foregoing Tune.

WHEN earth's foundation firſt was laid,
    By the Almighty Artiſt's hand,
By the Almighty Artiſt's hand,
'Twas then our perfect—our perfect laws were made,
Eſtabliſh'd by his ſtrict command.
    Hail! myſterious—hail! glorious Maſonry,
    That makes us ever great and free.

As man throughout for ſhelter fought,
In vain from place to place did roam,
In vain from place to place did roam,
Until from heaven—from heaven he was taught
To plan, to build, and fix his home.
    Hail! myſterious, &c.

From hence illuſtrious roſe our art,
And now it's beauteous piles appear,
And now it's beauteous piles appear,
Which ſhall to endleſs—to endleſs time impart,
How worthy and how great we are.
    Hail! myſterious, &c.

Nor we, leſs fam'd for ev'ry tye,
By which the human thought is bound,
By which the human thought is bound,
Love, truth, and friendſhip—and friendſhip ſocially,
Doth join our hearts and hands around.
    Hail! myſterious, &c.

Our actions, ſtill by virtue bleſt,
And to our precepts ever true,
And to our precepts ever true,
The world admiring,—admiring, ſhall requeſt
To learn, and our bright paths purſue.
    Hail! myſterious—hail! glorious Maſonry,
    That makes us great, and good, and free.

SONG CXI.

NO BODY.

If to force me to sing, it be your intention, Some one I will hint at, yet no body mention, no body, you'll cry, pshaw, that must be stuff, at singing I'm no body, That's the first proof.

Chorus.

No, no body, No, no body, No body, no body, no body, no.

No body's a name every body will own,
When something they ought to be asham'd of have done;
'Tis a name well apply'd to old maids and young beaus,
What they were intended for, no body knows.
    No, no body, &c.

If negligent servants should china-plate crack,
The fault is still laid on poor no body's back;
If accidents happen at home or abroad,
When no body's blam'd for it, is not that odd?
    No, no body, &c.

No body can tell you the pranks that are play'd,
When no body's by, betwixt master and maid:
She gently crys out, Sir, they'll some body hear us,
He softly replies, my dear, no body's near us.
    No, no body, &c.

But big with child proving, she's quickly discarded,
When favours are granted, no body's rewarded;
And when she's examin'd, crys, mortals, forbid it,
If I'm got with child, it was no body did it.
    No, no body, &c.

When by stealth the gallant the wanton wife leaves,
The husband affrighten'd, and thinks it is thieves;
He rouses himself, and crys loudly, Who's there?
The wife pats his cheek, and says, no body, dear.
    No, no body, &c.

Enough now of no body, sure has been sung,
Since no body's mention'd, nor no body's wrong'd;
I hope, for free speaking, I may not be blam'd,
Since no body's injur'd, nor no body's nam'd.
    No, no body, &c.

SONG CXII.
THE MAID IN BEDLAM.

One morning, very ear-ly; one morning, in

the spring, I heard a maid in Bedlam, who mourn-

ful-ly did sing, Her chains she rattl'd on her hands

while sweetly thus sung she, I love my love, because

I know, my love loves me.

Oh! cruel were his parents, who sent my love to sea;
And cruel, cruel, was the ship, that bore my love from me,
Yet I love his parents, since they're his, although they've ruin'd me.
 For I love my love, &c.

O ! fhould it pleafe the pitying pow'rs, to call me to the fky,
I'd claim a guardian angel's charge around my love to fly,
For to guard him from all dangers, how happy fhould I be?
  For I love my love, &c.

I'll make a ftrawy garland, I'll make it wondrous fine,
With rofes, lillies, daifies, I'll mix the eglantine:
And I will prefent it to my love, when he returns from fea.
  For I love my love, &c.

O if I were a little bird, to build upon his breaft;
Or if I were a nightingale, to fing my love to reft;
To gaze upon his lovely eyes, all my reward fhould be.
  For I love my love, &c.

O if I were an eagle, to foar into the fky,
I'd gaze around, with piercing eyes, where I my love might fpy:
But ah! unhappy maiden, that love you ne'er fhall fee.
  Yet I love my love, &c.

Whilft thus fhe fung, lamenting, her love was come on fhore,
He heard fhe was in Bedlam: then did he afk no more;
But ftraight he flew to find her, while thus replied he:
  I love my love, &c.

O Sir, do not affright me: are you my love, or not?
Yes, yes, my deareft Molly; I fear'd I was forgot.
But now I'm come to make amends for all your injury,
  And I love my love, &c.

SONG CXIII.

GRAMACHREE MOLLY.

To the foregoing Tune.

AS down on Banna's banks I ſtray'd, one evening
    in May,
The little birds, in blytheſt notes, made vocal ev'ry ſpray:
They ſung their little notes of love ; they ſung them
    o'er and o'er.
  Ah ! gramachree, mo challeenouge, mo Molly aſtore.

The daiſy pied, and all the ſweets the dawn of nature
    yields ;
The primroſe pale, the vi'let blue, lay ſcatter'd o'er the
    fields ;
Such fragrance in the boſom lies, of her whom I adore.
  Ah ! gramachree, &c.

I laid me down upon a bank, bewailing my ſad fate,
That doom'd me thus the ſlave of love, and cruel Mol-
    ly's hate.
How can ſhe break the honeſt heart, that wears her in
    it's core ?
  Ah ! gramachree, &c.

You ſaid you lov'd me, Molly dear; ah ! why did I be-
    lieve ?
Yea, who could think ſuch tender words were meant but
    to deceive ?
That love was all I aſk'd on earth ; nay heav'n could
    give no more.
  Ah ! gramachree, &c.

Oh! had I all the flocks that graze on yonder yellow hill,
Or low'd for me the num'rous herds, that yon green pastures fill,
With her I love I'd gladly share my kine and fleecy store,
  Ah! gramachree, &c.

Two turtle doves, above my head, sat courting on a bough,
I envy'd them their happiness to see them bill and coo;
Such fondness once for me she shew'd, but now, alas! 'tis o'er,
  Ah! gramachree, &c.

Then, fare thee well, my Molly dear? thy loss I still shall moan,
Whilst life remains in Strephon's heart, 'twill beat for thee alone.
Tho' thou art false, may heav'n on thee it's choicest blessings pour!
  Ah! gramachree, &c.

SONG CXIV.

To the foregoing Tune.

HAD I a heart for falsehood fram'd, I ne'er could injure you;
For tho' your tongue no promise claim'd, your charms wou'd make me true,
To you no soul shall bear deceit, no stranger offer wrong;
But friends in all the ag'd you'll meet, and lovers in the young.

But when they learn that you have bless'd another with your heart,
They'll bid aspiring passion rest, and act a brother's part,
Then, lady, dread not their deceit, no fear to suffer wrong;
For friends in all the ag'd you'll meet, and brothers in the young.

T

SONG CXV.
THE BOTTLE.

Whate'er squamish lovers may say, a mistress I've found to my mind; I enjoy her by night and by day, yet she grows still more lovely and kind: Of her beauties I never am cloy'd, tho' I constantly stick by her side, nor despise her because she's en-joy'd by a legion of lovers beside; For tho' thousands may broach her,

Should I try to describe all her merit,
　　With her praises I ne'er should have done ;
She's brimful of sweetness and spirit,
　　And sparkles with freedom and fun :
Her stature's majestic and tall,
　　And taper her bosom and waist,
Her neck long, her mouth round and small,
　　And her lips how delicious to taste !
　　　　For tho', &c.

You may grasp her with ease by the middle,
　　To be open'd how vast her delight,
And yet her whole sex is a riddle,
　　You never can stop her too tight ?
When your instrument you introduce,
　　To her circle and magical power,
Pop away from within flies the juice,
　　And your senses are drown'd in the shower.
　　　　For tho', &c.

But the sweetest of raptures that flow
　　From the bountiful charmer I prize,
Is sure when her head is laid low,
　　And her bottom's turn'd up to the skies :
Stand to her and fear not to win her,
　　She'll never prove peevish or coy,
And the farther and deeper you're in her,
　　The fuller she'll fill you will joy.
　　　　For tho', &c.

Thus naked and clasp'd in my arms,
　　With her my sweet moments I'd spend,
And revel the more on her charms,
　　When I share her delight with a friend :
To divinity, physic, or law,
　　Her favours I never shall grudge,
Tho' each night she may make a *faux pas*
　　With the bishop, the doctor, or judge,
　　　　For tho', &c.

MISCELLANY. 221

SONG CXVI.
JAMIE GAY.

Affectuoso.

As Jamie Gay gae'd blythe his way, A-
long the banks of Tweed, A bon-ny lass
as e-ver was, came tripping o'er the
mead. The hear-ty swain, un-taught
to feign--, the buxom nymph survey'd; and, full of glee, as lad could be,
be-spoke the blooming maid.

Dear laffie, tell, why by thy-fell
  Thou lonely wander'ſt here ?
My ewes, ſhe cry'd, are ſtraying wide ;
  Canſt tell me, laddie, where ?
To town I hie, he made reply,
  Some pleaſing ſport to ſee :
But thou'rt ſo neat, ſo trim, ſo ſweet,
  I'll ſeek thy ewes with thee.

She gave her hand, nor made a ſtand ;
  But lik'd the youth's intent :
O'er hill and dale, o'er plain and vale,
  Right merrily they went.
The birds ſang ſweet, the pair to greet,
  And flow'rets bloom'd around ;
And as they walk'd, of love they talk'd,
  And lovers joys when crown'd.

And now the ſun had roſe to noon,
  The zenith of his power,
When, to the ſhade, their ſteps they made,
  To paſs the mid-day hour.
The bonny lad row'd in his plaid,
  The laſs, who ſcorn'd to frown :
She ſoon forgot the ewes ſhe ſought,
  And he to gang to town.

SONG CXVII.

ALL YE WHO WOU'D WISH.

All ye who wou'd wiſh to ſucceed with a laſs,

learn how the affair's to be done; For if

you ſtand fooling and ſhy, like an aſs, you'll looſe

her, looſe her, You'll looſe her, as ſure as a

gun.

With whining, and ſighing, and vows, and all that,
    As far as you pleaſe you may run;
She'll hear you, and jeer you, and give you a pat,
    But jilt you, jilt you,
She'll jilt you, as ſure as a gun.

To worſhip, and call her bright goddeſs is fine,
  But mark you the conſequence, mum:
The baggage will think herſelf realy divine,
  And ſcorn you, ſcorn you,
She'll ſcorn you as ſure as a gun.

Then be with a maiden bold, frolic, and ſtout,
  And no opportunity ſhun;
She'll tell you ſhe hates you, and ſwear ſhe'll cry out.
  But mum—mum—
But mum—ſhe's as ſure as a gun.

SONG CXVIII.

HE STOLE MY TENDER HEART AWAY.

The fields were green, the hills were gay, and

birds were ſinging on each ſpray, When Colin met

me in the grove, and told me tender tales of

love Was ever fwain fo blythe as he, fo kind,

fo faithful, and fo free, in fpite of all my

friends cou'd fay, young Colin ftole my heart away, in

fpite of all my friends cou'd fay, young Colin ftole my

heart away.

When ere he trips the meads along,
He fweetly joins the woodlark's fong;
And when he dances on the green,
There's none fo blythe as Colin feen:
If he's but by I nothing fear,
For I alone am all his care;

Then ſpite of all my friends can ſay,
He's ſtole my tender heart away.

My mother chides when ere I roam,
And ſeems ſurpris'd I quit my home:
But ſhe'd not wonder that I rove,
Did ſhe but feel how much I love;
Full well I know the gen'rous ſwain,
Will never give my boſom pain;
Then ſpite of all my friends can ſay,
He's ſtole my tender heart away.

SONG CXIX.

THE YOUNG MAN's WISH.

Free from the buſtle, care, and ſtrife, Of this

ſhort va - rie - ga - ted life, O let me ſpend my days,

In rural ſweetneſs with a friend, To whom my

mind I may unbend, Nor cenſure, heed or praiſe.

Nor cenſure, heed, or praiſe.

Riches bring cares—I aſk not wealth,
Let me enjoy but peace and health,
   I envy not the great;
'Tis theſe alone can make me bleſt,
The riches take of eaſt and weſt,
   I claim not theſe or ſtate.

Tho' not extravagant nor near,
But through the well spent checker'd year,
  I'd have enongh to live;
To drink a bottle with a friend,
Assist him in distress, ne'er lend,
  But rather freely give.

I too would wish, to sweeten life,
A gentle, kind, good natur'd wife,
  Young sensible and fair,
One who could love but me alone,
Prefer my cot to e'er a throne,
  And sooth my every care.

Thus happy with my wife and friend,
My life I cheerfully would spend,
  With no vain thoughts opprest;
If heav'n has bliss for me in store,
O grant me this, I ask no more,
  And I am truly blest.

SONG CXX.
THE THING.

Fine songsters apologies too often use, when

call'd on I'm ready to sing; With hums, or with

haws ne'er attempt to refuse, And egad, Sirs, I'll

give you the thing, the thing, and egad, Sirs, I'll give

you the thing.

Conceited our beaux arm in arm walk the street,
  In idleness take their full swing;
Each levels his glass, when a lady they meet,
  And if handsome, they swear she's the thing.

Thus at Smithfield, the Jocky his nag will commend,
  What a shape, why he's fit for the king;
He's found, wind and limb, on the word of a friend,
  And for spirits—he's really the thing.

With smile of self-interest, the landlord imparts,
  Butt-entire I always do bring;
Old stingo, I draw, that will cherish your hearts,
  And in flavour indeed 'tis the thing.

See Jenny with Jocky to playhouse repair,
  Miss Brent to hear warble and sing;
Pretenders to music they praise ev'ry air,
  With I vow and protest she's the thing.

The sportsman with joy views the hare in full speed,
  In ecstacy hears the sky ring;
With cry of the hounds, and of each neighing steed,
  And in transport he cries 'tis the thing.

The prude her own person consults in the glass,
  Admiring her finger and ring;
Then concludes that her beauty all others surpass,
  And that man must confess she's the thing.

Jack Tar full of glee to the garden will stroll,
  In search, Sirs, of something like !—g;
There boards on Moll Jenkins, and swears by his soul,
  She's rig'd fore and aft, quite the thing.

The parson well pleas'd trims the smoaking Sir Loin,
  And slyly leers at the pudding;
Lord bless me, he cries, how nobly I dine,
  O pudding and beef is the thing.

But clasp'd in the arms of a good natur'd pair,
  With mutual embraces we cling;
That enjoyment alone dispells ev'ry care,
  Which you all must allow is the thing.

SONG CXXI.
THE BRITISH GRENADIERS.

Some talk of Alexander, and some of Hercu-

les, of Conon, and Lysander, and some Miltia-

des; but of all the world's brave heroes, there's none

that can compare, with a tow, row, row, row, row, to

Chorus.

the British grenadiers. But of all the world's brave

heroes, there's none that can compare, with a tow

row, row, row, row, to the British grenadiers.

None of those ancient heroes e'er saw a cannon ball,
Or knew the force of powder to flay their foes withal;
But our brave boys do know it, and banifh all their fears,
With a tow, row, row, row, row, the Britifh grenadiers.
    But our brave boys, &c.

When e'er we are commanded to ftorm the palifades,
Our leaders march with fufees and we with hand grenades
We throw them from the glacis about our enemies ears,
With a tow, row, row, row, row, the Britifh grenadiers.
    We throw them, &c.

The god of war was pleafed, and great Bellona fmiles,
To fee thefe noble heroes, of our Britifh ifles;
And all the gods celeftial, defcending from their fpheres,
Beheld with admiration the Britifh Grenadiers.
    And all the goods celeftal, &c.

Then let us crown a bumper, and drink a health to thofe,
Who carry caps and pouches that wear the louped cloaths,
May they and their commanders, live happy all their years,
With a tow, row, row, row, row, the Britifh grenadiers.
    May they and their commanders, &c.

SONG CXXII.

ONE BOTTLE MORE.

Assist me ye lads, who have hearts void of guile,

to sing in the praises of old Ireland's isle;

Where true ho-spi-ta-li-ty o-pens the door,

And friendship detains us for one bottle more,

one bottle more, arrah, one bottle more, And

friendship detains, us for one bottle, more.

U iij

Old England, your taunts on our country forbear;
With our bulls, and our brogues, we are true and sincere,
For if but one bottle remain'd in our store,
We have generous hearts, to give that bottle more.

In Candy's, in Church-street, I'll sing of a sett
Of six Irish blades who together had met;
Four bottles a piece made us call for our score.
And nothing remained but one bottle more.

Our bill being paid, we were loath to depart,
For friendship had grappled each man by the heart;
Where the least touch you know makes an Irishman roar
And the whack from shilella, brought six bottles more.

Slow Phœbus had shone thro' our window so bright,
Quite happy to view his blest children of light,
So we parted, with hearts neither sorry nor sore,
Resolving next night to drink twelve bottle more.

SONG CXXIII.

Tune—*Ally Croaker*—Page 203.

THRO' the fiery flames of love, I'm in a sad taking,
I'm smock'd like a hog, that's hung up for bacon,
My stomach 'tis scorch'd, like an over-done mutton-chop,
That of good gravie, wont yield you one single drop.
 O love, love, love is like a giddiness,
 That wont let a poor man gang about his business.

My great guts, and little guts, is burnt to a cinder;
As a hot burning-glass, burns a dishclout to tinder,
As cheese, by a hot salamander is toasted,
By the beauty of your cheeks, like mutton I am roasted;
 O love, &c.

Come all you young men, who after ladies dandle,
I'm girlt like a duck's-foot, sing'd over a candle,
By this, and by 'tother, I m treated uncivil,
Like a gizard I am pepper'd, and then made a *Devil*.
 O love, &c.

The warblers are heard in the grove,
  The linnet, the lark, and the thrush,
The blackbird and sweet cooing dove,
  With music enchant every bush.
Come, let us go forth to the mead,
  Let us see how the primroses spring ;
We'll lodge in some village on Tweed,
  And love while the feather'd folks sing.

How does my love pass the lang day ?
  Does Mary not tend a few sheep ?
Do they never carlessly stray,
  While happily she lies asleep ?
Tweed's murmurs should lull her asleep ;
  Kind nature indulging my bliss,
To relieve the saft pains of my breast,
  I'd steal an ambrosial kiss.

'Tis she does the virgin excel,
  No beauty with her may compare ;
Love's graces around her do dwell :
  She's fairest where thousands are fair.
Say, charmer, where do the flocks stray,
  Oh ! tell me at noon where they feed ;
Shall I seek them on sweet winding Tay,
  Or the pleasanter banks of the Tweed.

SONG CXXV.

To the foregoing Tune.

WHEN Maggy and me were acquaint,
   I carry'd my noddle fu' hie,
Nae lintwhite on all the gay plain,
   Nor goudſpink ſae bonny as ſhe.
I whiſtled, I pip'd, and I ſang,
   I woo'd, but I came nae great ſpeed,
Therefore I maun wander abroad,
   And lay my banes over the Tweed.

To Maggy my love I did tell,
   Saut tears did my paſſion expreſs;
Alas! for I lo'ed her o'er well,
   And the women lo'ed ſic a man leſs.
Her heart, it was frozen and cauld,
   Her pride had my ruin decreed,
Therefore I will wander abroad,
   And lay my banes far frae the Tweed.

SONG CXXVI.
FOUR AND TWENTY FIDDLERS.

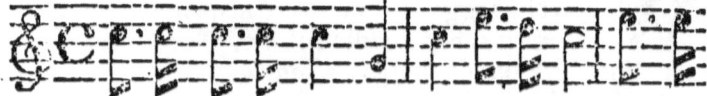

Four and twenty fid-lers all on a row, Four and

twenty fid-lers all on a row, there was fiddle fad-

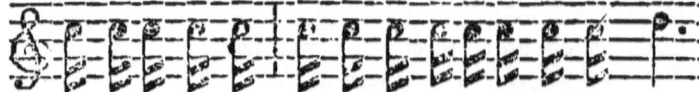

dle fiddle and my double damme femi quible down

below.   It is my lady's holiday, there-

fore let us be mer-ry.

2 Four and twenty drummers all on a row, there was hey rub a dub ho rub a dub fiddle faddle, &c.

3 Four and twenty trumpeters all on a row, there was tantara rara tantara rera hey rub a dub, &c.

4 Four and twenty coblers all on a row, there was flab awl and cobler and cobler and flab awl tantara rera, &c.

5 Four and twenty fencing masters all on row, there was push carte and teirce down at heel cut him acrofs, stab awl and cobler, &c.

6 Four and twenty captains all on a row, there was Oh! d—n me kick him down stairs push carte and teirce, &c.

7 Four twenty parsons all on a row, there was Lord have mercy upon us, O! d—n me kick him down stairs, &c.

8 Four and twenty taylors all on a row, one caught a loufe, another let it loofe and another cried knock him down with the goofe, Lord have merey upon us, &c.

9 Four and twenty barbers all on a row, there was bag whigs, short bobs, toupees, long ques, shave for a penny, Oh d—n'd hard times two ruffles and ne'er a shirt, one caught a loufe, &c.

10 Four and twenty Quakers, all on a row, there was Abraham begat Isaac, and Isaac begat Jacob, and Jacob peopled the twelve tribes of Israel, with bag wigs, short bobes, toupees, long ques, shave for a penny, Oh d—n'd hard times two ruffles and ne'er a shirt, one caught a loufe, another ler it loofe, and another cried knock him down with the goofe, Lord have mercy upon us, Oh d—n me kick him down stairs, push carte and teirce, down at heel cut him acrofs, stab awl and cobler, and cobler and stab awl, tantara rera, tantara rera, hey rub a dub, ho rub a dub, fiddle faddle fiddle and my double damme semi quibble down below, It is my lady's holiday, therefore let us be merry.

X

SONG CXXVII.
THE LASS OF PEATIE's MILL.

Her arms, white, round, and smooth;
  Breasts rising in their dawn;
To age it would give youth,
  To press them with his hand.
Through all my spirits ran
  An extasy of bliss,
When I such sweetness fand,
  Wrapt in a balmy kiss.

Without the help of art,
  Like flow'rs which grace the wild,
Her sweets she did impart,
  Whene'er she spoke or smil'd.
Her looks, they were so mild,
  Free from affected pride,
She me to love beguil'd;
  I wish'd her for my bride.

O! had I all that wealth
 Hoptouns high mountains fill,
Infur'd long life and health,
 And pleafure at my will;
I'd promife, and fulfil,
 That none but bonny fhe,
The lafs of Peatie's mill,
 Should fhare the fame with me.

SONG CXXVIII.

FROM THE EAST BREAKS THE MORN.

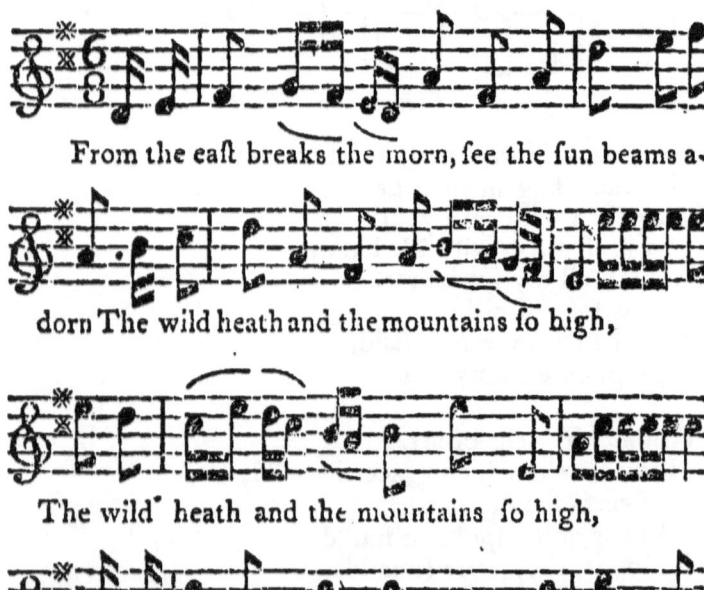

From the eaft breaks the morn, fee the fun beams a-

dorn The wild heath and the mountains fo high,

The wild heath and the mountains fo high,

Shrilly opes the ftaunch hound, the fteed neighs to

the found, And the floods and the valleys re - - - - - - -

ply, And the floods and the valleys re-ply.

Our forefathers, fo good,
   Prov'd their greatnefs of blood,
By encount'ring the pard and the boar,
   Ruddy health bloom'd the face,
   Age and youth urg'd the chace,
And taught woodlands and forefts to roar.

   Hence of noble defcent,
   Hills and wilds we frequent,
Where the bofom of nature's reveal'd,
   Tho' in life's bufy day,
   Man of man make a prey,
Still let ours be the prey of the field.

   With the chace in full fight,
   Gods how great the delight,
How our mutual fenfations refine,
   Where is care, where is fear,
   Like the winds in the rear,
And the man's loft in fomething divine.

   Now to horfe, my brave boys,
   Lo each pants for the joys,
That anon fhall enliven the whole,
   Then at eve we'll difmount,
   Toils and pleafures recount,
And renew the chace over the bowl.

SONG CXXIX.

To the foregoing Tune.

LET gay ones and great,
   Make the moſt of their fate,
From pleaſure to pleaſure they run,
   Well who cares a jot,
   I envy them not,
While I have my dog and gun.

   For exerciſe air
   To the field I repair,
With ſpirits unclouded and light :
   The bliſſes I find
   No ſtings leave behind,
But health and diverſion unite.

SONG CXXX.

RAIL NO MORE.

Rail no more, ye learned aſſes, 'Gainſt the joys

the bowl ſupplies; Sound it's depth, and fill your

Draw the scene for wit and pleasure;
  Enter jollity and joy;
We for thinking have no leisure;
  Manly mirth is our employ.
Since in life there's nothing certain,
  We'll the present hour engage;
And, when death shall drop the curtain,
  With applause we'll quit the stage.

SONG CXXXI.
THE PLOWMAN.

The plowman he's a bonny lad, his mind is e-ver true, O, His garters tied below his knee, his bonnet it is blue, O. *Chorus.* Then up wi't a' my plowman lad, O hey, the merry plowman, o

a' the lads that e'er I saw, commend me to the

plowman.

As I was walking in a field,
  I chanc'd to meet a plowman,
I told him I would learn to till,
  If that he would prove true man.
    Then up wi't a', &c.

He said, my dear, take you no fear,
  But I will do my best, O!
I'll study for to pleasure thee,
  As I have done the rest, O.
    Then up wi't a', &c.

My oufen they are stout and good,
  As ever labour'd ground, O!
The foremost ox is lang and sma',
  The others firm and round, O.
    Then up wi't a' &c.

So he with speed did yoke his plough,
  And with a gad was driven,
But when he came between the stilts,
  He thought he was in heaven.
    Then up wi't a', &c.

The foremost ox fell in a fur,
  The other's then did founder,

The plowman lad he breathlefs grew,
 In troth it was nae wonder.
  Then up wi't a', &c.

Plowing once upon a hill,
 Below there was a flane, O!
Which gard the fire flee frae the fock,
 The plowman gied a grane, O!
  Then up wi't a', &c.

'Tis I have tilled meikle ground,
 I've plowed faugh and fallow,
He that will not drink the plowman's health,
 Is but a faucy fellow.
  Then up wi't a', &c.

SONG CXXXII.

COME ON, MY BRAVE TARS.

Come on my brave tars, let's away to the wars,

To honour and glory advance; For

now we've beat Spain, let us try this campaign, To

humble the pride of old France, my brave boys, to hum-

ble the pride of old France.

See William, brave prince,
A true blue ev'ry inch,
Who will honour th' illustrious name:
 May he conqueror be
 O'er our empire the sea,
And transmit British laurels to fame,
 My brave boys, &c.

Three heroes combin'd,
When the dons they could find,
Vied who ſhould be foremoſt in battle;
By no lee ſhore affrighted,
Altho' they're benighted,
They made Britiſh thunder to rattle,
Brave boys, &c.

See Dalrymple, Prevoſt,
Gallant Barrington too,
And Farmer who glorioufly fell:
With brave Pearſon, all knew
That the hearts of true blue,
Once rouz'd, not the world could excell,
My brave boys, &c.

With ſuch heroes as thoſe,
Tho' we've numberleſs foes,
Britiſh valour refplendant ſhall ſhine:
And we ſtill hope to ſhow
That their pride will be low,
In eighty, as fam'd fifty-nine,
My brave boys, &c.

Then brave lads enter here,
And partake of our cheer,
You ſhall feaſt and be merry and ſing:
With the grog at your noſe,
Drink ſucceſs to true blues,
Huzza! and ſay God ſave the king,
My brave boys, &c.

SONG CXXXIII.
THE FLOWERS OF EDINBURGH.

Slow.

My love was once a bon-ny lad, he was
the flower of all his kin, the abfence of
his bon-ny face, has rent my ten-der heart
in twain. I day nor night find
no delight, in fi-lent tears I ftill complain, and exclaim 'gainft thofe my rival foes,
that hae ta'en from me my darling fwain.

Despair and anguish fills my breast,
  Since I have lost my blooming rose;
I sigh and moan while others rest,
  His absence yield me no repose.
To seek my love I'll range and rove,
  Thro' ev'ry grove and distant plains
Thus I'll ne'er cease, but spend my days,
  T' hear tidings from my darling swain.

There's nothing strange in nature's change,
  Since parents shew such cruelty;
They caus'd my love from me to range,
  And knows not to what destiny.
The pretty kids and tender lambs
  May cease to sport upon the plain;
But I'll mourn and lament, in deep discontent,
  For the absence of my darling swain.

Kind Neptune, let me thee intreat,
  To send a fair and pleasant gale;
Ye dolphins sweet, upon me wait,
  And do convey me on your tail.
Heav'ns bless my voyage with success,
  While crossing of the raging main,
And send me safe o'er to that distant shore,
  To meet my lovely darling swain.

All joy and mirth at our return
  Shall then abound from Tweed to Tay;
The bells shall ring, and sweet birds sing,
  To grace and crown our nuptial day.
Thus bless'd with charms in my love's arms,
  My heart once more I will regain;
Then I'll range no more to a distant shore,
  But in love will enjoy my darling swain.

MISCELLANY. 255

SONG CXXXIV.
PLATO's ADVICE.

Says Pla--to, why should man be vain? Since bounteous heav'n has made him great, Why looketh he with insolent disdain On those undeck'd with wealth or state? Can splendid robes, or beds of down, or costly gems that deck the fair, Can all the glo - ries of a crown, Give health, or ease the brow of care?

256   THE MUSICAL

The fcepter'd king, the burthen'd flave,
   The humble, and the haughty, die ;
The rich, the poor, the bafe, the brave,
   In duft, without diftinction, lie ;
Go, fearch the tombs where monarchs reft,
   Who once the greateft titles bore :
The wealth and glory they poffefs'd,
   And all their honours, are no more.

So glides the meteor through the fky,
   And fpreads along a gilded train ;
But, when it's fhort-liv'd beauties die,
   Diffolves to common air again.
So 'tis with us, my jovial fouls !—
   Let friendfhip reign while here we ftay ;
Let's crown our joys with flowing bowls,—
   When Jove us calls we muft away.

SONG CXXXV.

JOHNNY's GREY BREEKS.

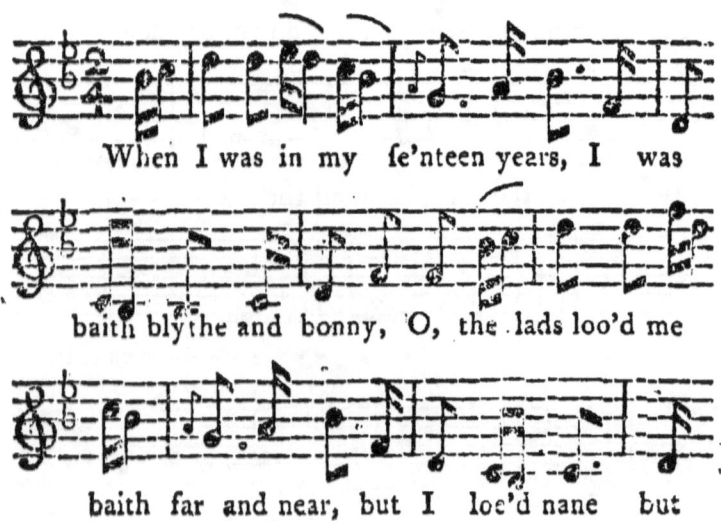

When I was in my fe'nteen years, I was baith blythe and bonny, O, the lads loo'd me baith far and near, but I loe'd nane but

He was a handsome fellow,
　　His humour was baith frank and free,
His bonny locks fae yellow,
　　Like gou'd they glitter'd in my ee';
His dimpl'd chin and rosy cheeks,
　　And face so fair and ruddy, O,
And then a days his grey breeks,
　　Was neither auld nor duddy, O.

But now they are thread bare worn,
　　They're wider than they wont to be,
They're tashed like, and fair torn,
　　And clouted fair on ilka knee.
But gin I had a summer's day,
　　As I have had right mony, O,
I'll make a web o' new grey,
　　To be breeks to my Johnny, O.

For he's well wordy o' them,
　　And better gin I had to gi'e,
And I'll tak pains upo' them,
　　Frae fau'ts I'll strive to keep them free.
To clead him weel shall be my care,
　　And please him a' my study, O,
But he maun wear the auld pair,
　　A wee, tho' they be duddy, O,

For when the lad was in his prime,
　　Like him there was nae mony, O,
He ca'd me aye his bonny thing,
　　Say, wha wou'd nae lo'e Johnny, O.
So I lo'e Johnny's grey breeks,
　　For a' the care they've gi'en me yet,
And gin we live anither year,
　　We'll keep them hail between us yet.

Now to conclude his grey breeks,
　　I'll sing them up wi' mirth and glee;
Here's luck to all the grey steeks,
　　That shows themselves upo' the knee,

And if wi' health I'm spaired,
  A wee while as I wish I may,
I shall hae them prepared,
  As well as ony that's o' grey.

SONG CXXXVI.

To the foregoing Tune.

NOW smiling spring again appears,
  With all the beauties of her train,
Love soon of her arrival hears,
  And flies to wound the gentle swain.
How gay does nature now appear,
  The lambkins frisking o'er the plain,
Sweet feather'd songsters now we hear,
  While Jenny seeks her gentle swain.

Ye nymphs, Oh! lead me thro' the grove,
  Thro' which your streams in silence mourn;
There with my Johnny let me rove,
  'Till once his fleecy flock return;
Young Johnny is my gentle swain
  That sweetly pipes along the mead,
So soon's the lambkins hear his strain,
  With eager steps return in speed.

The flocks now all in sportive play
  Come frisking round the piping swain,
Then fearful of too long delay,
  Run bleating to their dams again,
Within the fresh green myrtle grove,
  The feather'd choir in rapture sing,
And sweetly warble forth their love,
  To welcome the returning spring.

SONG CXXXVII.

SAE MERRY AS WE TWA HAE BEEN.

Slow.

A lass that was laden'd with care, sat hea-vi-ly under yon thorn, I listen'd a while for to hear, When thus she be-gan for to mourn: Whene'er my dear shepherd was there, the birds did melodiously sing, and cold nipping winter did wear a face that re-sembled the spring. Sae merry as we twa

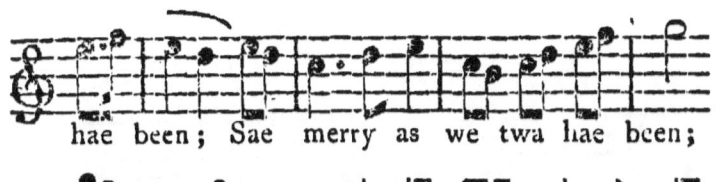

Our flocks feeding close by his side,
  He gently pressing my hand,
I view'd the wide world in it's pride,
  And laugh'd at the pomp of command!
My dear, he wou'd aft to me say,
  What makes you hard-hearted to me;
Oh! why do you thus turn away,
  From him wha is dying for thee?
Sae merry, &c.

But now he is far from my sight,
  Perhaps a deceiver may prove,
Which makes me lament day and night,
  That ever I granted my love,
At eve, when the rest of the folk
  Were merrily seated to spin,
I set myself under an oak,
  And heavily sighed for him.
Sae merry, &c.

SONG CXXXVIII.
THE BANKS OF THE DEE.

'Twas summer and softly the breezes were

blowing, and sweetly the nightingale sung from the

tree, at the foot of a rock where the river was

flowing, I sat myself down on the banks of the Dee.

Flow on, lovely Dee, flow on thou sweet river, thy

banks purest stream shall be dear to me ever, for

there I first gain'd the affection and favour of

Jamie the glo-ry and pride of the Dee.

But now he's gone from me, and left me thus mourning,
To quell the proud rebels, for valiant is he ;
And ah ! there's no hopes of his speedy returning,
To wander again on the Banks of the Dee.
He's gone, helpless youth ! o'er the rude roaring billows ;
The kindest and sweetest of all the gay fellows ;
And left me to stray 'mong'st the once loved willows,
The loneliest maid on the Banks of the Dee.

But time, and my prayers, may perhaps yet restore him ;
Blest peace may restore my dear shepherd to me ;
And when he returns, with such care I'll watch o'er him,
He never shall leave the sweet Banks of the Dee.
The Dee then shall flow, all it's beauties displaying ;
The lambs on it's banks shall again be seen playing ;
While I, with my Jamie, am carelessly straying,
And tasting again all the sweets of the Dee.

ADDITIONS BY A LADY.

THUS sung the fair maid on the banks of the river,
And sweetly re-echo'd each neighbouring tree ;
But now all these hopes must evanish for ever,
Since Jamie shall ne'er see the Banks of the Dee.
On a foreign shore the sweet youth lay dying,
In a foreign grave his body's now lying ;
While friends and acquaintance in Scotland are crying
For Jamie the glory and pride of the Dee.

Mishap on the hand by which he was wounded ;
Mishap on the wars that call'd him away
From a circle of friends by which he was surrounded,
Who mourn for dear Jamie the tedious day.

Oh! poor haplefs maid, who mourns difcontented,
The lofs of a lover fo juftly lamented;
By time, only time, can her grief be contented,
And all her dull hours become cheerful and gay.

'Twas honour and bravery made him leave her mourning,
From unjuft rebellion his country to free;
He left her, in hopes of his fpeedy returning
To wander again on the Banks of the Dee.
For this he defpis'd all dangers and perils;
'Twas thus he efpous'd Britannia's quarrels,
That when he came home he might crown her with laurels,
The happieft maid on the Banks of the Dee.

But fate had determin'd his fall to be glorious,
Though dreadful the thought muft be unto me;
He fell, like brave Wolfe, where the troops were victorious,
Sure each tender heart muft bewail the decree:
Yet, though he is gone, the once faithful lover,
And all our fine fchemes of true happinefs over,
No doubt he implored his pity and favour
For me he had left on the Banks of the Dee.

SONG CXXIX.

To the foregoing Tune.

ALL you that are wife and think life worth enjoying,
Or foldier or failor, by land or by fea,
In loving and laughing your time be employing;
Your glafs to your lip and your lafs on your knee.
Come fing away, honeys, and caft off all forrow!
Though we all die to-day let's be merry to morrow;
A hundred years hince 'twill be loo late to borrow
A moment of time to be joyous and free!
 Then fing, &c.

My lord and the bifhop, in fpite of their fplindor,
When death gives the call, from their glories muft part;
Your beautiful dame, whin the fummons is fent her,
Will feel the blood ebb from the cheek to the heart.
Then fing away, honeys, and caft off your forrow!
Though you all die to-day, yet be merry to morrow!
A hundred years hince 'twill be too late to borrow
A cordial to cherifh the forrowful heart!
 Then fing, &c.

For riches and honour, then, why all this riot,
Your wrangling and jangling, and all your alarms?
Arrah! burn you, my honeys, you'd better be quiet,
And take, while you can, a kind girl, to your arms.
You'd better be finging and cafting off forrow!
Though you all die to-day, fure, be merry to-morrow!
A hundred years hince 'twill be too late to borrow
One moment to toy and enjoy her fweet charms!
 You'd better, &c.

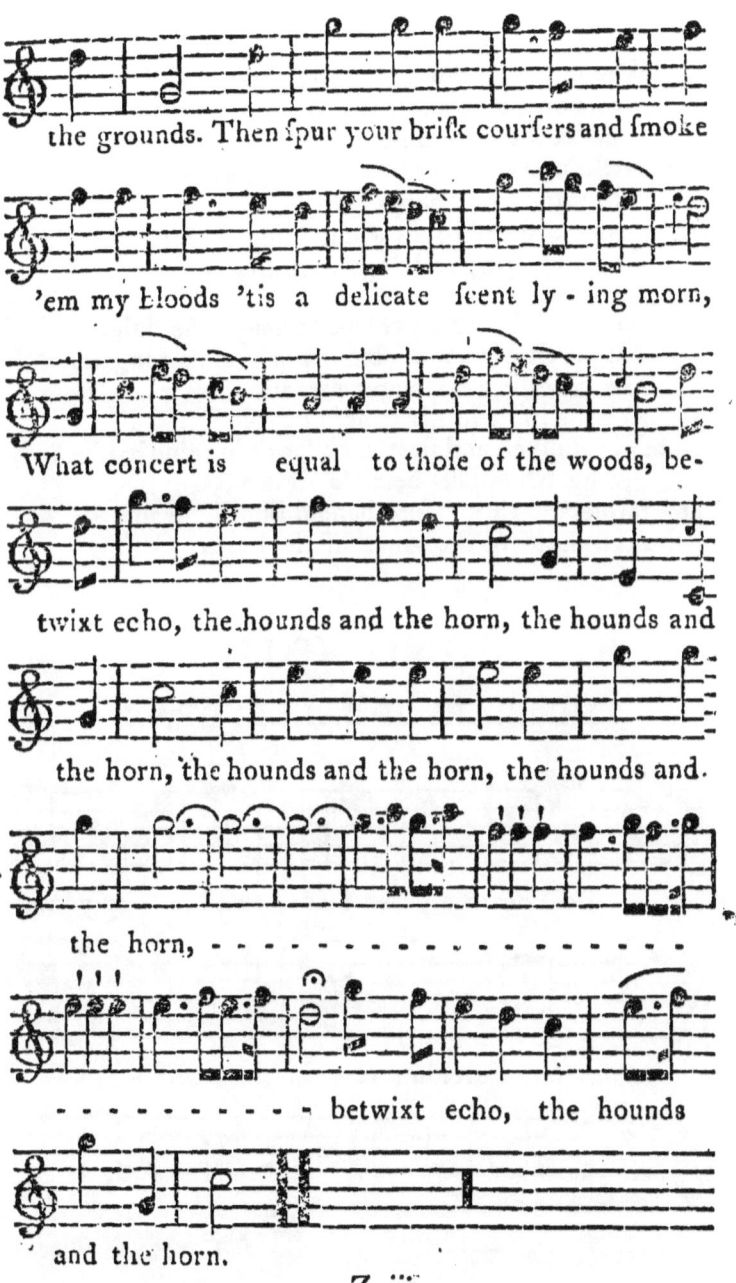

Each earth see he tries at in vain,
  The cover no safety can find,
So he breaks it and scowers amain,
  And leaves us at distance behind;
O'er rocks and o'er rivers and hedges we fly,
  All hazard and danger we scorn;
Stout Reynard we'll follow until that he die,
  Cheer up the good dogs with the horn.

And now he scarce creeps through the dale,
  All parch'd from his mouth hangs his tongue,
His speed can no longer prevail,
  Nor his life can his cunning prolong;
From our staunch and fleet pack 'twas in vain that he fled,
  See his brush falls bemir'd forlorn,
The farmers with pleasure behold him lie dead,
  And shout to the sound of the horn.

SONG CXLI.

THE BRAES OF BALLENDEAN.

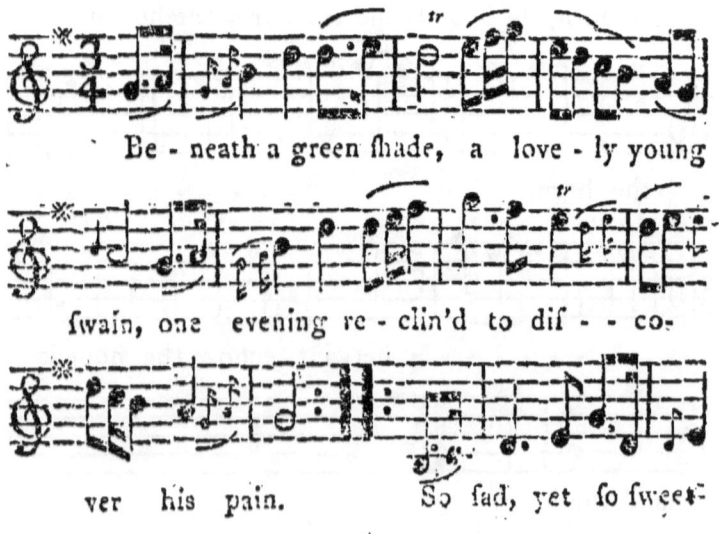

Be-neath a green shade, a love-ly young swain, one evening re-clin'd to dif--co-ver his pain. So sad, yet so sweet-

MISCELLANY.

ly he warbled his woe; The winds ceas'd to breathe, and the fountains to flow, Rude winds with compassion could hear him complain; yet Chloe less gentle, was deaf to his strain.

How happy he cry'd, my moments once flew,
E'er Chloe's bright charms first flash'd in my view!
These eyes, then, with pleasure, the dawn could survey;
Nor smil'd the fair morning more cheerful than they.
Now, scenes of distress please only my sight:
I sicken in pleasure, and languish in light.

Thro' changes, in vain, relief I pursue:
All, all, but conspire, my griefs to renew:
From sunshine, to zephyrs and shades, we repair;
To sunshine we fly from too piercing an air:

Z iij

But love's ardent fever burns always the fame;
No winter can cool it, no fummer inflame.

But, fee the pale moon, all clouded, retires!
The breezes grow cool, not Strepon's defires!
I fly from the dangers of tempeft and wind;
Yet nourifh the madnefs that preys on my mind.
Ah, wretch! how can life thus merit thy care,
Since length'ning it's moments but lengthens difpair?

SONG CXLII.

WHAT POSIES AND ROSES.

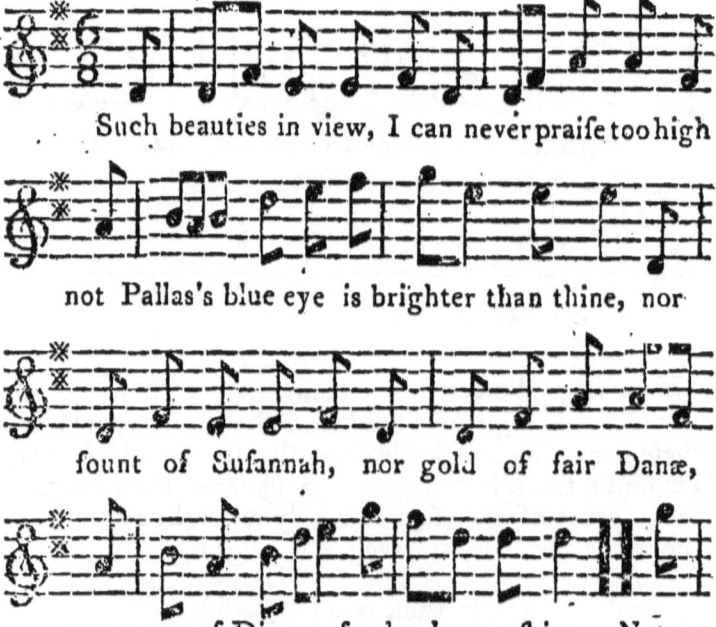

Such beauties in view, I can never praife too high
not Pallas's blue eye is brighter than thine, nor
fount of Sufannah, nor gold of fair Danæ,
nor moon of Dianna fo clearly can fhine. Not

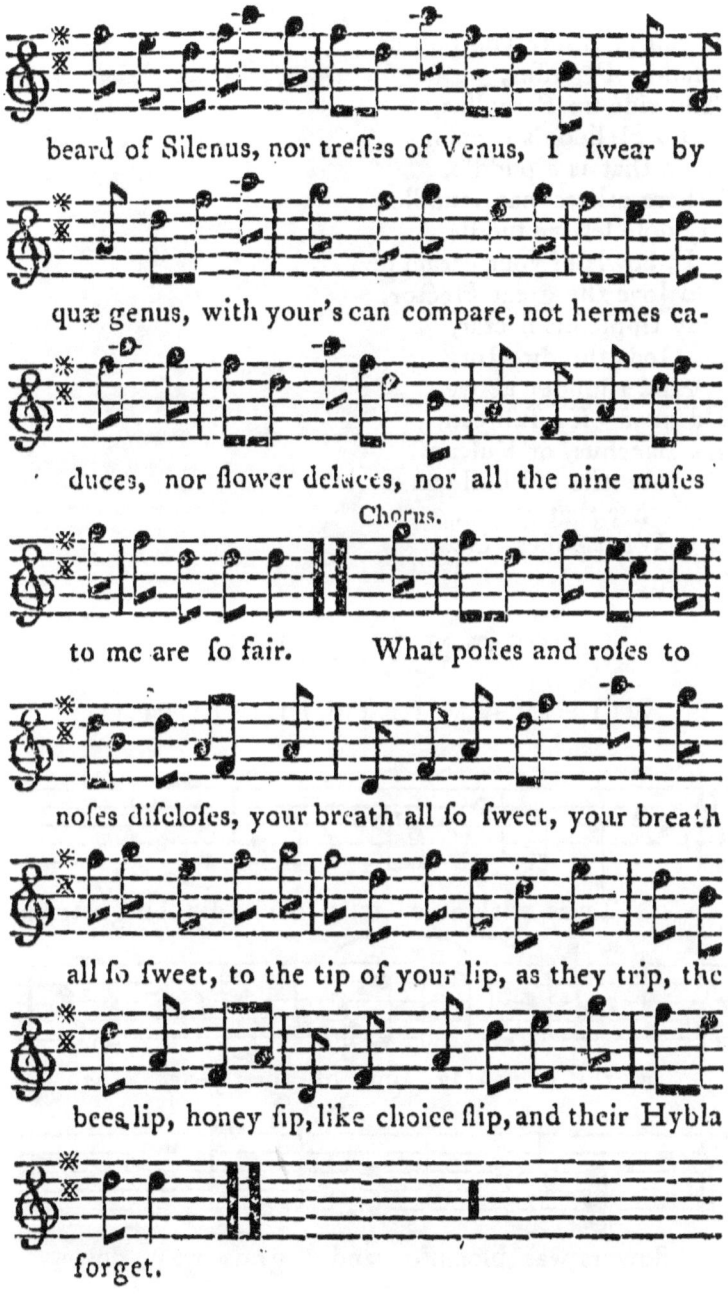

When girls like you pafs us
I faddle Pegaffus,
And ride up Parnaffus,
    To Helicon's ftream.
Even that is a puddle,
Where others may muddle;
My nofe let me fuddle
    In bowls of your cream!
Old Jove the great Hector,
May tipple his nectar,
Of Gods the director,
    And thunder above:
I'd quaff off a full can,
As Bacchus, or Vulcan,
Or Jove the old bull can
    To her that I love.
        What pofies, &c.

SONG CXLIII.

WITHIN A MILE OF EDINBURGH.

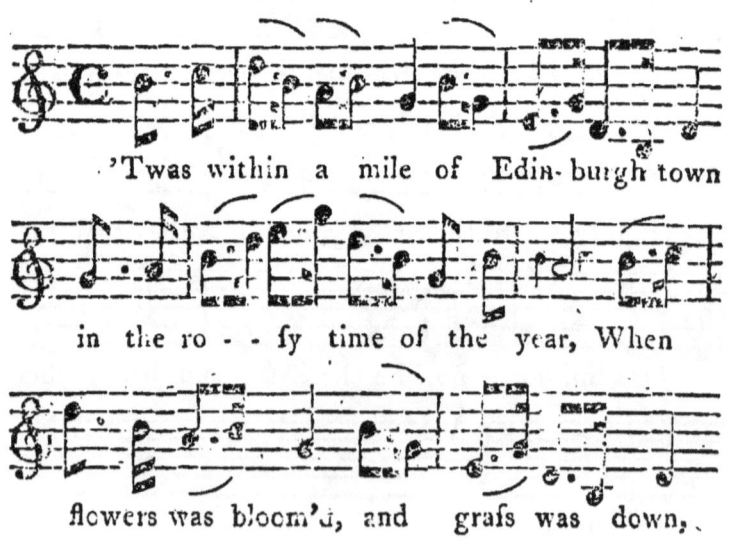

'Twas within a mile of Edinburgh town in the ro- -fy time of the year, When flowers was bloom'd, and grafs was down,

O Jocky was a wag, that never wou'd wed,
Though long he had followed the lafs,
Contented fhe work'd, and eat her brown bread,
And merrily turn'd up the grafs.
   Bonny Jocky blythe and gay,
   Won' her heart right merrily,
   But ftill fhe blufh'd, and frowning faid,
     I cannot, &c.

But when that he vow'd he wou'd make her his bride,
Tho' his herds and his flocks were not few,
She gave him her hand and a kifs befides,
And vow'd fhe'd for ever be true.
   Bonny Jocky blythe and gay,
   Won' her heart right merrily,
   At church fhe no more frowning faid,
     I cannot, &c.

SONG CXLIV.

Tune—Fy gar rub her o'er wi' ftrae—Page 29.

DEAR Roger, if your Jenny geck,
   And anfwer kindnefs wi' a flight,
Seem unconcern'd at her neglect:
   For women in a man delight;
But them defpife who're foon defeat,
   And wi' a fimple face give way:
To a repulfe—Then be not blate;
   Pufh bauldly on, and win the day.

When maidens, innocently young,
   Say aften what they never mean,
Ne'er mind their pretty lying tongue,
   But tent the language of their een:
If thefe agree, and fhe perfift
   To anfwer a' your love with hate,
Seek elfewhere to be better bleft,
   And let her figh when it's too late.

SONG CXLV.
THIS COLD FLINTY HEART.

This cold flin-ty heart, it is you who have warm'd, You waken'd my paſſions, my ſen-ſes have charm'd, You waken'd my paſſions, my ſen- - -ſes have charm'd. In vain againſt me-rit and Cy-mon I ſtrove, What's life without paſſion, ſweet paſ-ſion of love, ſweet paſ-ſion, ſweet paſſion, ſweet paſ-ſion of love.

The froſt nips the buds, and the roſe cannot blow,
From the youth that is froſt nipp'd no rapture can flow,
Elyſium to him but a deſert will prove,
What's life without paſſion, ſweet paſſion of love.

The ſpring ſhould be warm, the young ſeaſon be gay,
Her birds and her flow'rets make blithſome ſweet May,
Love bleſſes the cottage and ſings thro' the grove,
What's life without paſſion, ſweet paſſion of love.

MISCELLANY. 277

SONG CXLVI.
LEWIS GORDON.

Very slow.

Oh! send Lewis Gordon hame, And the lad I winna name; Tho' his back be at the wa' Here's to him that's far a-wa' *Chorus.* Oh hon! my Highlandman, Oh! my bonny Highlandman, weel wou'd I my true love ken, a-mang ten thou-sand Highlandmen.

A a

Oh to fee his tartan trews,
Bonnet blue, and laigh heel'd fhoes,
Philebeg aboon his knee,
That's the lad that I'll gang wi'.

The princely youth that I do mean,
Is fitted for to be a king:
On his breaft he wears a ftar,
You'd take him for the god of war.

Oh, to fee this princely one,
Seated on a royal throne;
Difafters a' wou'd difappear,
Then begins the jub'lee year,

SONG CXLVII.
TULLOCHGORUM.

Fiddlers, your pins in temper fix,
And rofet weel your fiddle-fticks;
But banifh vile Italian tricks
    Frae out your quorum:
Nor *forte*'s wi' *piano*'s mix,
    Gie's *Tullochgorum*.

FERGUSSON.

Come gie's a fang, the lady cry'd, and lay your difputes all afide, what nonfenfe is't for folks to chide, for what's been done before them.

Tullochgorum's my delight,
It gars us a' in ane unite,
And ony fumph that keeps up fpite,
  In confcience I abhor him.
Blithe and merry we's be a',
Blithe and merry, blithe and merry,
Blithe and merry we's be a',
  To make a chearfu' quorum.

Blithe and merry we's be a',
As lang's we ha'e a breath to draw,
And dance, till we be like to fa',
   The reel of Tullochgorum.

There needs na' be so great a phrase
Wi' dringing dull Italian lays,
I wadna gi'e our ain Strathspeys
   For half a hundred score o'm.
They're douff and dowie at the best,
Douff and dowie, douff and dowie,
They're douff and dowie at the best,
   Wi' a' their variorum.
They're douff and dowie at the best,
Their allegro's, and a' the rest,
They cannot please a Highland taste,
   Compar'd wi' Tullochgorum.

Let warldly minds themselves oppress
Wi' fear of want, and double cess,
And silly fauls themselves distress
   Wi' keeping up decorum,
Shall we sae sour and sulky sit,
Sour and sulky, sour and sulky,
Shall we sae sour and sulky sit,
   Like auld Philosophorum?
Shall we sae sour and sulky sit,
Wi' neither sense, nor mirth, nor wit,
And canna rise to shake a fit
   At the reel of Tullochgorum.

My choicest blessings still attend
Each honest-hearted open friend,
And calm and quit be his end,
   Be a' that's good before him!
May peace and plenty be his lot,
Peace and plenty, peace and plenty,
May peace and plenty be his lot,
   And dainties a great store o' em!

May peace and plenty be his lot,
Unftain'd by any vicious blot!
And may he never want a groat
   That's fond of Tullochgorum.

But for the difcontented fool,
Who wants to be oppreffion's tool,
May envy gnaw his rotten foul,
   And blackeft fiends devore him!
May dole and forrow be his chance,
Dole and forrow, dole and forrow,
May dole and forrow be his chance,
   And honeft fouls abhore him!
May dole and forrow be his chance,
And a' the ills that come frae France,
Whoe'er he be that winna dance
   The reel of Tullochgorum!

SONG CXLVIII.
THE YELLOW HAIR'D LADDIE.

In April, when primroses paint the sweet plain, and sum-mer ap-proach-ing, re-joiceth the swain. joiceth the swain, The Yellow hair'd Laddie wou'd often-times

go, To wilds and deep glens, where the hawthorn trees grow. hawthorn trees grow.

There, under the shade of an old sacred thorn,
With freedom, he sung his loves, evening and morn.
He sang with so soft and inchanting a sound,
That Sylvans and Fairies, unseen, danc'd around.

The shepherd thus sung: tho' young Maddie be fair,
Her beauty is dash'd with a scornful, proud air:
But Susie was handsome, and sweetly could sing;
Her breath, like the breezes. perfum'd in the spring.

That Maddie, in all the gay bloom of her youth,
Like the moon, was inconstant, and never spoke truth:
But Susie was faithful, good humour'd, and free,
And fair as the goddess that sprung from the sea.

That mamma's fine daughter, with all her great dow'r,
Was aukwardly airy, and frequently four:
Then, fighing, he wifh'd, would parents agree,
The witty, fweet Sufie, his miftrefs might be.

SONG CXLIX.

To the foregoing Tune.

FROM THE GENTLE SHEPHERD.

PEGGY.

WHEN firft my dear laddie gade to the green hill,
And I at ewe-milking firft fey'd my young fkill,
To bear the milk-bowie, nae pain was to me,
When I at the bughting forgather'd with thee.

PATIE.

When corn-rigs wav'd yellow, and blue heather-bells
Bloom'd bonny on moorland and fweet rifing fells,
Nae birns, briers, or breckens gave trouble to me,
If I found the berries right ripen'd for thee.

PEGGY.

When thou ran, or wreftled or putted the ftane,
And came aff the victor, my heart was ay fain,
Thy ilka fport manly gave pleafure to me;
For nane can putt, wreftle, or run fwift as thee.

PATIE.

Our Jenny fings faftly the Cowden-broom-knows,
And Rofie lilts fweetly the Milking the ewes;

There's few Jenny Nettles, like Nancy, can sing ;
At—Thro' the wood, laddie, Bess gars our lugs ring.

But when my dear Peggy sings, with better skill,
The Boatman, Tweedside, or the Lass of the mill,
'Tis mony times sweeter and pleasant to me ;
For tho' they sing nicely, they cannot like thee.

P E G G Y.

How easy can lassies trow what they desire !
When praising sae kindly increases love's fire :
Give me still this pleasure, my study shall be,
To make myself better, and sweeter, for thee.

SONG CL.
HAD NEPTUNE.

Had Neptune, when first he took charge of the sea, been as wife, or at least been as merry as we, he'd have thought better o'nt, and instead of the brine, would have fill'd the vast ocean with ge-ne-rous wine — would have fill'd the vast ocean with ge-ne-rous wine.

What trafficking then would have been on the main,
For the fake of good liquor, as well as for gain,
No fear then of tempeſt, or danger of ſinking,
The fiſhes ne'er drown that are always a-drinking.

The hot thirſty ſun would drive with more haſte,
Secure in the evening of ſuch a repaſt;
And when he'd got tipfey, wou'd have taken his nap,
With double the pleaſure in Thetis's lap.

By the force of his rays, and thus heated with wine,
Confider how glorioufly Phœbus would ſhine,
What vaſt exhalations he'd draw up on high,
To relieve the poor earth as it wanted fupply.

How happy us mortals, when bleſt with ſuch rain,
To fill all our veſſels, and fill 'em again,
Nay even the beggar that has ne'er a diſh,
Might jump in the river and drink like a fiſh.

What mirth and contentment, on every one's brow,
Hob as great as a prince, dancing after his plough,
The birds in the air as they play on the wing,
Altho' they but fip would eternally fing.

The ſtars, who I think, don't to drinking incline,
Would friſk and rejoice at the fume of the wine;
And merrily twinkling would foon let us know,
That they were as happy as mortals below.

Had this been the cafe, what had we enjoy'd,
Our ſpirits ſtill rifing our fancy ne'er cloy'd;
A pox then on Neptune, when 'twas in his pow'r,
To ſlip like a fool, ſuch a fortunate hour.

WE'RE GAILY YET.

SONG CLI.

There was a lad, and they cau'd him Dick;
He gae me a kifs, and I bit his lip;
And down in the garden he fhew'd me a trick;
And we're no very fou, but we're gaily yet.
    And we're gaily yet, &c.

There were three lads, and they were clad;
There were three laffes, and them they had.
Three trees in the orchard are newly fprung;
And we's a get geer enough, we're but young.
    And we're gaily yet, &c.

Now fye, John Thomson, rin,
Gin ever ye ran in your life;
De'el get ye, but hye, my dear Jock;
There's a man got to bed with your wife.
    Then up wi't Ailey, &c.

Then away John Thomson ran,
And I true he ran with speed;
But, before he had run his length,
The false loon had done the deed.
    Then up wi't Ailey, &c.
    (End with the first verse:
We're gaily yet, and we're gaily yet, &c.)

SONG CLII.

BUSH ABOON TRAQUAIR.

Hear me, ye nymphs, and ev-e-ry swain, I'll
tell how Peggy grieves me, tho' thus I languish
and complain, A-las! she ne'er believes me.
My vows and sighs, like si-lent air, un-heed-

ed, ne-ver move her, The bon-ny Bush a-boon Tra-quair, was where I first did love her.

That day she smil'd, and made me glad,
  No maid seem'd ever kinder :
I thought myself the luckiest lad,
  So sweetly there to find her.
I try'd to soothe my am'rous flame,
  In words that I thought tender ;
If more there pass'd I'm not to blame,
  I meant not to offend her.

Yet now she scornful flees the plain,
  The fields we then frequented ;
If e'er we meet, she shews disdain,
  She looks as ne'er acquainted.
The bonny bush bloom'd fair in May,
  It's sweet's I'll ay remember ;
But now her frowns make it decay,
  It fades as in December.

Ye rural pow'rs, who hear my strains,
  Why thus should Peggy grieve me ?
Oh ! make her partner in my pains,
  And let her smiles relieve me :

B ij

If not, my love will turn despair;
  My passion no more tender;
I'll leave the bush aboon Traquair,
  To lonely wilds I'll wander.

SONG CLIII.

To the foregoing Tune.

AT setting day, and rising morn,
  Wi' soul that still shall love thee,
I'll ask of heav'n thy safe return,
  Wi' a' that can improve thee.
I'll visit aft the Birken-bush,
  Where first thou kindly tald me
Sweet tales of love, and hid my blush
  Whilst round thou didst infald me.

To a' our haunts I will repair,
  To Greenwood-shaw or fountain,
Or where the summer day I'd share
  Wi' thee upon yon mountain.
There will I tell the trees and flow'rs,
  From thoughts unfeign'd and tender,
By vows you're mine, by love is yours
  A heart which cannot wander.

SONG CLIV.

AMYNTA.

My sheep I've forsaken, and left my sheep-

Through regions remote in vain do I rove,
And bid the wide ocean secure me of love;
O fool to imagine that ought can subdue,
A love so well founded, a passion so true!
    O what had my youth, &c.

Alas! 'tis too late at thy fate to repine;
Poor shepherd, Amynta no more can be thine;
Thy tears are all fruitless, thy wishes are vain;
The moments neglected return not again.
    O what had my youth with ambition to do?
    Why left I Amynta? why broke I my vow?
    O give me my sheep, and my sheep-hook restore,
    And I'll wander from love and Amynta no more.

SONG CLVI.

THE GALLANT SAILOR.

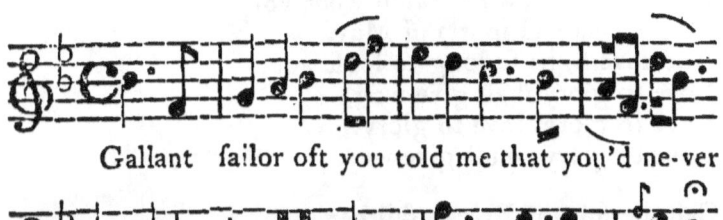

Gallant sailor oft you told me that you'd never

leave your love, To your vows I now must hold you

now's the time your love to prove to your vows I now

must hold you, now's the time your love to prove.

SAILOR.

Is not Britain's flag degraded,
Have not Frenchmen brav'd our fleet?
How can sailors live upbraided,
While the Frenchmen dare to meet;
How can sailors live upbraided,
While the Frenchmen dare to meet.

NAN.

Hear me, gallant sailor, hear me,
While your country has a foe,
He is mine too, never fear me,
I may weep but you must go;
I may weep, I may weep,
I may weep, but you shall go.

SAILOR.

Though this flow'ry season woos you
To the peaceful sports of May,
And love sighs so long to loose you,
Love to glory shall give way,
Love to glory, love to glory,
Love to glory, must give way.

Can the sons of Britain fail her,
While her daughters are so true;
Your soft courage must avail her,
We love honour loving you,
We love honour, we love honour,
We love honour loving you.

BOATSWAIN.

War and danger now invite us,
Blow ye winds, auspicious blow;
Ev'ry gale will most delight us
That can waft us to the foe,
Ev'ry gale will most delight us,
That can waft us to the foe.

SONG CLVIII.

ON FRIENDSHIP.

The world, my dear Myra, is full of deceit,

and friendship's a jewel we seldom can meet.

How much to be priz'd and esteem'd is a friend,
On whom we may always with safety depend;
Our joys when extended will always increase,
And griefs when divided are hush'd into peace.
When fortune is smiling what crouds will appear,
Their kindness to offer and friendship sincere,
Yet change but the prospect and point out distress,
No longer to court you they eagerly press.

SONG CXLIX.

THE SEIGE OF TROY.

Proud Paris, despising fair Helen's great pomp, he ventur'd the foaming bil-lows to jump, for her fa la lal de ral lal; And came to Troy with a numerous train, whereof the great-

est part was slain, for her fa la lal de ral lal de ral, Whereof the greatest part was slain, for her fa la lal de ral lal.

Menelau's enrag'd at such a great loss,
With a thousand ships the ocean did cross,
    For her fa la, &c.
And steer'd on his course, tho' the seas they did roar,
Queen Nell's bright charms drew his ships to the shore,
    Of her fa la, &c.

Agamemnon regardless of his country's harms,
Dispatch'd to Achilles two heralds at arms,
    For her fa la, &c.
But stern Achilles he threw down his shield,
And swore by his sceptre, he'd ne'er take the field
    For the loss of her fa la, &c.

Ulysses renowned for prudence and wit,
He feign'd himself crazy, to stick by the butt
    Of Penelope's fa la, &c.
And plow'd up the sand with an ass and a hog,
A rare pretension to keep him *in. cog.*
    To manure her fa la, &c.

But Hector may curse it, and so may his Sire,
For *it* was the *thing*, that set Troy on fire,
    Her fa la, &c.
And himself to be drag'd round the town by the heels,
At stern Achilles's chariot wheels,
    For her fa la, &c.

But stern Achilles, he falling in love,
With Priam's fair daughter, which did his death prove,
    Her fa la, &c.
For cunningly Paris shot him in the heel,
With a poisoned arrow made of the fine steel.
    For her fa la, &c.

SONG CLX.
ROSLIN CASTLE.

'Twas in that season of the year, when all things gay and sweet appear, that Colin with the morning ray, arose and sung his rural lay. Of Nanny's charms the shepherd sung, the hills and dales with Nanny rung, while Roslin castle heard the swain and echo'd, back the cheerful strain.

Awake, sweet muse! the breathing spring,
With rapture warms; awake and sing;
Awake, and join the vocal throng,
Who hail the morning with a song;
To Nanny raise the cheerful lay;
O! bid her haste and come away;
In sweetest smiles herself adorn,
And add new graces to the morn.

O hark, my love! on ev'ry spray,
Each feather'd warbler tunes his lay;
'Tis beauty fires the ravish'd throng;
And love inspires the melting song:
Then let my raptur'd notes arise:
For beauty darts from Nanny's eyes;
And love my rising bosom warms,
And fills my soul with sweet alarms,

O! come, my love! thy Colin's lay
With rapture calls, O come away!
Come, while the muse this wreathe shall twine
Around that modest brow of thine:
O! hither haste, and with thee bring
That beauty blooming like the spring,
Those graces that divinely shine,
And charm this ravish'd breast of mine!

SONG CLXI.

To the foregoing Tune.

FROM Roslin castle's echoing walls
Resounds my shepherd's ardent calls,
My Colin bids me come away,
And love demands I should obey.
His melting strain and tuneful lay
So much the charms of love display,
I yield—nor longer can refrain,
To own my love, and bless my swain.

No longer can my heart conceal
The painful pleasing flame I feel,
My soul retorts the am'rous strain,
And echoes back in love again,
Where lurks my songster? from what grove
Does Colin pour his notes of love?
O bring me to the happy bow'r,
Where mutual love may bliss secure.

Ye vocal hills that catch the song,
Repeating, as it flies along,
To Colin's ear my strain convey,
And say, I haste to come away.
Ye zephyrs soft that fan the gale,
Waft to my love the soothing tale;
In whispers all my soul express,
And tell, I haste his arms to bless.

SONG CLXII.
JOHN O' BADENYON.

When first I came to be a man, of twenty years or so, I thought myself a handsome youth, And fain the world wou'd know, in best attire I stept abroad, with spirits brisk and gay, and here and there, and every where, was like a morn in May. No care I had, nor fear of want, but

rambled up and down, and for a beau I might have pafs'd, in country or in town; I ftill was pleas'd where'er I went, and when I was alone, I tun'd my pipe, and pleas'd myfell, wi' John o'

Badenyon.

Now in the days of youthful prime,
   A miftrefs I muft find;
For love they fay, gives one an air,
   And ev'n improves the mind:
On Phillis fair, above the reft,
   Kind fortune fix'd my eyes,
Her piercing beauty ftruck my heart,
   And fhe became my choice:
To Cupid then, with hearty pray'r,
   I offer'd many a vow,
And danc'd and fung, and figh'd and fwore,
   As other lovers do:

But when at laſt I breath'd my flame,
  I found her cold as ſtone ;
I left the girl, and tun'd my pipe
  To John of Badenyon.

When love had thus my heart beguil'd,
  With fooliſh hopes and' vain,
To friendſhip's port I ſteer'd my courſe,
  And laugh'd at lovers' pain ;
A friend I got by lucky chance,
  'Twas ſomething like divine ;
A honeſt friend's a precious gift,
  And ſuch a gift was mine :
And now, whatever might betide,
  A happy man was I,
In any ſtrait I knew to whom
  I freely might apply :
A ſtrait ſoon came, my friend I try'd,
  He laugh'd and ſpurn'd my moan :
I hy'd me home, and pleas'd myſelf
  With John of Badenyon.

I thought I ſhould be wiſer next,
  And would a patriot turn ;
Began to doat on Johnny Wilkes,
  And cry up Parſon Horne :
Their noble ſpirit I admir'd,
  And prais'd their manly zeal,
Who had, with flaming tongue and pen,
  Maintain'd the public weal ;
But 'ere a month or two was paſt,
  I found myſelf betray'd ;
'Twas ſelf and party after all,
  For all the ſtir they made.
At laſt I ſaw theſe factious knaves
  Inſult the very throne ;
I curs'd them all, and tun'd my pipe
  To John of Badenyon.

What next to do I mus'd a while,
   Still hoping to succeed,
I pitch'd on books for company,
   And gravely try'd to read;
I bought and borrow'd ev'ry where,
   And study'd night and day;
Nor mist what dean or doctor wrote,
   That happen'd in myway:
Philosophy I now esteem'd.
   The ornament of youth,
And carefully, thro' many a page,
   I hunted after truth:
A thousand various schemes I try'd,
   And yet was pleas'd with none;
I threw them by, and tun'd my pipe
   To John of Badenyon.

And now, ye youngsters, ev'ry where,
   Who want to make a show,
Take heed in time, nor vainly hope
   For happiness below;
What you may fancy pleasure here,
   Is but an empty name;
For girls, and friends, and books, and so,
   You'll find them all the same.
Then be advis'd, and warning take,
   From such a man as me,
I'm neither Pope nor Cardinal,
   Nor one of low degree,
You'll find displeasure ev'ry where:
   Then do as I have done,
E'en tune your pipe, and please yourself
   With John of Badenyon.

SONG CLXIII.
THE WAND'RING SAILOR.

The wand'ring sailor ploughs the main. a competence in life to gain, Undaunted braves the stormy seas, To find at last content and ease, To find at last content and ease, In hopes when toil and danger's o'er, To anchor on his native shore, In hopes when toil and danger's o'er, To anchor on his native shore, to anchor

* When round the bowl the jovial crew,
The early scenes of youth renew,
Tho' each his fav'rite fair will boast,
This is the universal toast :
This is the universal toast :

  May we when toil and danger's o'er,
  Cast anchor on our native shore,
  May we when toil and danger o'er,
  Cast anchor on our native shore,
  Cast anchor on his native shore.

  * *These words to be sung to the first part of the tune.*

SONG CLXIV.
HIGHLAND QUEEN.

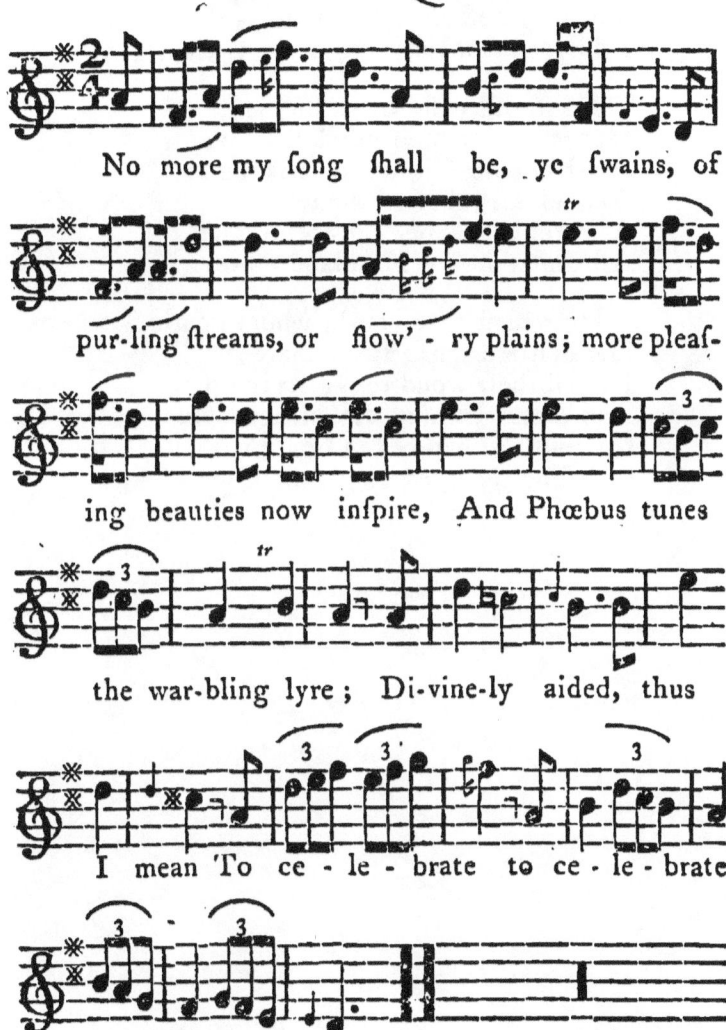

No more my song shall be, ye swains, of pur-ling streams, or flow'-ry plains; more pleaf-ing beauties now infpire, And Phœbus tunes the war-bling lyre; Di-vine-ly aided, thus I mean To ce-le-brate to ce-le-brate my Highland Queen.

In her, sweet innocence you'll find,
With freedom, truth, and beauty join'd;
From pride and affectation free,
Alike she smiles on you and me,
The brightest nymph that trips the green,
I do pronounce my Highland Queen.

No sordid wish, or trifling joy,
Her settled calm of mind destroy;
Strict honour fills her spotless soul,
And adds a lustre to the whole;
A matchless shape, a graceful mien,
All center in my Highland Queen.

How blest that youth, whom gentle Fate
Has destin'd for so fair a mate;
Has all these wond'rous gifts in store,
And each returning day brings more:
No youth so happy can be seen,
Possessing thee, my Highland Queen.

SONG CLXV.

MAN MAY ESCAPE.

Man may escape from rope or gun, nay some have

outliv'd the doctor's pill: Who takes a woman

must be undone, that ba-sil-isk is sure to

kill. The fly that sips treacle is lost in the

sweets, so he that tastes woman, woman, woman,

he that tastes woman, ruin meets.

314   THE MUSICAL

SONG CLXVI.
TALLY HO.

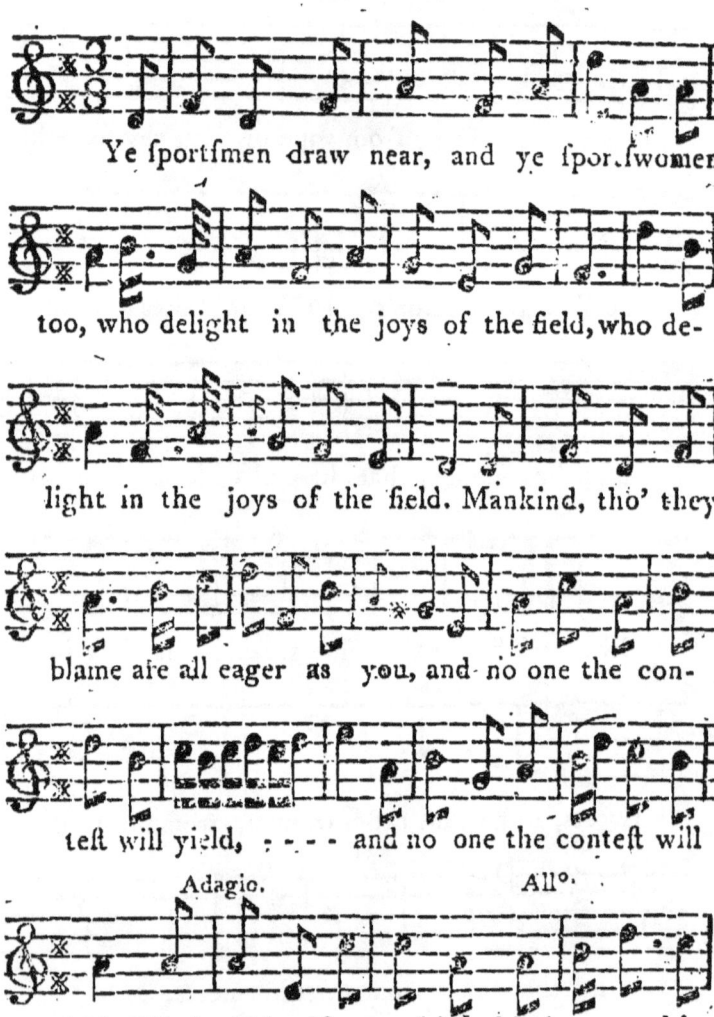

Ye sportsmen draw near, and ye sportswomen too, who delight in the joys of the field, who delight in the joys of the field. Mankind, tho' they blame are all eager as you, and no one the contest will yield, - - - and no one the contest will yield. His lordship, his worship, his honour, his

The lawyer will rife with the firft of the morn
  To hunt for a mortgage or deed;
The hufband gets up at the found of the horn
  And rides to the commons full fpeed;
The patriot is thrown in-purfuit of his game;
  The poet too often lays low,
Who, mounted on Pegafus, flies after fame,
  With hark forward, huzza, Tally ho.

While fearlefs o'er hills and o'er woodlands we fweep,
  Tho' prudes on our paftime may frown,
How oft do they decency's bounds overleap,
  And the fences of virtue break down?
Thus public, or private, for penfion, for place,
  For amufement, for paffion, for fhow,
All ranks and degrees are engag'd in the chace,
  With hark forward, huzza, Tally ho.

MISCELLANY.   317

SONG CLXVII.
THE AULD GOODMAN.

O late in an evening forth I went, a little before the sun gae'd down, and there I chanc'd by accident, to light on a battle new begun. A man and his wife, was fa'n in a strife, I can-na' weel tell you how it began, but ay she wail'd her wretched life, and cry'd ever, Alake, my auld goodman.

He.

Thy auld goodman that thou tells of,
  The country kens where he was born,
Was but a filly poor vagabond,
  And ilka ane leugh him to fcorn;
For he did fpend, and make an end
  Of gear that his forefathers wan,
He gart the poor ftand frae the door,
Sae tell nae mair of thy auld goodman.

She.

My heart alake, is liken to break,
  When I think on my winfome John,
His blinkin eye, and gate fae free,
  Was naething like thee, thou dofen'd drone.
His rofie face, and flaxen hair,
  And a fkin as white as ony fwan,
Was large and tall, and comely withal,
  And thou'lt never be like my auld goodman.

He.

Why doft thou pleen? I thee maintain,
  For meal and mawt thou difna want;
But thy wild bees I canna pleafe,
  Now when our gear 'gins to grow fcant.
Of houfehold ftuff thou haft enough,
  Thou wants for neither pot nor pan;
Of fiklike ware he left thee bare,
  Sae tell nae mair of thy auld goodman.

She.

Yes, I may tell, and fret myfell,
  To think on thefe blyth days I had,
When he and I together lay
  In arms into a well-made bed;

But now I sigh and may be sad,
   Thy courage is cauld, thy colour wan,
Thou falds thy feet, and fa's asleep,
   And thou'lt ne'er be like my auld goodman.

Then coming was the night sae dark,
   And gane was a' the light o' day;
The carl was fear'd to miss his mark,
   And therefore wad nae langer stay;
Then up he gat, and he ran his way,
   I trow the wife the day she wan,
And ay the oe'rword of the fray
   Was ever, Alake, my auld goodman.

SONG CLXVIII.

TODLEN HAME.

When I have a saxpence un-der my thumb,
then I'll get credit in ilk-a town, but ay
when I'm poor, they bid me gae bye, O poverty parts
good com-pa-ny. Todlen hame, Todlen hame,
O cou'dna my love come todlen hame.

Fair fa' the goodwife, and fend her good sale,
She gi'es us white bannocks to drink her ale,
Syne if that her tippony chance to be sma',
We'll tak a good scour o't. and ca't awa'.
    Todlen hame, todlen hame,
    As round as a neep come todlen hame.

My kimmer and I lay down to sleep,
And twa pint-stoups at our bed's feet;
And ay when we waken'd, we drank them dry:
What think ye of my wee kimmer and I?
    Todlen butt, and todlen ben,
    Sae round as my love comes todlen hame.

Leez me on liquor, my todlen dow,
Ye're ay sae good-humour'd when weeting your mou';
When sober, sae four, ye'll fight with a flee,
That 'tis a blyth sight to the bairns and me,
    When todlen hame, todlen hame,
    When round as a neep you come todlen hame.

SONG CLXIX.

BY JOVE I'LL BE FREE.

Come, all ye young lovers, who wan with despair, com-

pose idle sonnets and sigh for the fair; who puff up

their pride by enhancing their charms, and tell them

'tis heaven to lie in their arms: be wise by example;

take pattern from me; For, let what will happen,

by Jove I'll be free, by Jove I'll be free; For, let

what will happen, by Jove I'll be free.

Young Daphne I saw, in the net soon was caught;
I ly'd and I flatter'd, as custom has taught:
I prefs'd her to blifs, which fhe granted full foon;
But the date of my paffion expir'd with the moon.
She vow'd fhe was ruined; I faid it might be;
I'm forry, my dear: but by Jove I'll be free.

The next was young Phyllis, as bright as the morn;
The love that I proffer'd fhe treated with fcorn;
I laugh'd at her folly, and told her my mind,
That none can be handfome but fuch as are kind.
Her pride and ill nature were loft upon me:
For, in fpite of fair faces, by Jove I'll be free.

Let others call marriage the harbour of joys;
Calm peace I delight in, and fly from all noife;
Some choofe to be hamper'd, 'tis fure a ftrange rage,
And, like birds, they fing beft when they're put in a cage;
Confinement's the devil; 'twas not made for me;
Let who will be bound-flaves, by Jove I'll be free.

Then let the brifk bumper run over the glafs,
In a toaft to the young and the beautiful lafs,
Who, yielding and eafy, prefcribes no dull rule,
Nor thinks it a wonder a lover fhould cool.
Let us bill like the fparrow, and rove like the bee;
For, in fpite of grave leffons, by Jove I'll be free.

SONG CLXXI.

FAREWELL, YE GREEN FIELDS.

Fare-well, ye green fields and sweet groves, where Phillis engag'd my fond heart, where nightingales warble their loves, and nature is dress'd without art. No pleasure ye now can afford, nor music can lull me to rest; for Phillis proves false to her word, and Strephon can never be blest.

E e

Oftimes by the fide of a fpring,
Where rofes and lillies appear,
Gay Phillis of Strephon would fing,
For Strephon was all fhe held dear.
But foon as fhe found by my eyes,
The paffion that glow'd in my breaft,
She then to my grief and furprife,
Prov'd all fhe had faid was a jeft.

Too late to my forrow I find,
The beauties alone that will laft,
Are thofe that are fix'd in the mind,
Which envy or time cannot blaft.
Beware then, beware how ye truft,
Coquets who to love make pretence,
For Phillis to me had been juft,
If nature had blefs'd her with fenfe.

SONG CLXXII.

To the foregoing Tune.

THOUGH wifdom will preach about joy, Sir,
   Truth, folly will practife as well;
Man is fimple, and life's but a toy, Sir,
In toying it is we excel.
Is it worth our while, for learning to toil,
To labour, to love, and to think,
Thought ne'er was defign'd to trouble the mind,
So only let's mind who's to drink.

King Solomon, (I'm not profane, Sir,)
Was a wife, yet a whimfical one,
He never thought any thing vain, Sir,
'Till once that his pleafure was gone.
He ufed to fay, there's a time to play,
To labour, to love, and to think.
Let thofe in their prime, remember their time,
At prefent it's time we fhou'd drink.

A pox on reflection, be jolly,
Dispassionate dulness despise,
Did you once know the pleasure of folly,
You'd ne'er be so weak to be wise.
Let the trumpet of Fame, those heroes proclaim,
Who never at Cannon-ball blink,
Let the busy in trade, be *cent*. per *cent*. made,
'Tis *cent*. per *cent*. better to drink.

Come, about with a bumper, boys, hearty,
To our king and our country, success;
Toast oblivion to envy and party,
May freedom our fire-sides bless.
Here's a health to all those, who will face our foes,
To those who dare speak as they think,
To such sort of men, again and again,
Again and again let us drink.

SONG CLXXIII.

BLOW HIGH, BLOW LOW.

Blow high, blow low, let tempefts tear, the main-

maft by the board, My heart with thoughts of thee my

dear, and love well ftor'd, fhall brave all danger, fcorn

all fear, the roaring winds the raging fea, in hopes

on fhore to be once more, fafe moor'd with thee.

A-loft while mountains high we go, the whiftling

winds that fcud along, and the furge roaring from be-

SONG CLXXIV.

RUSSEL's TRIUMPH.

Thursday in the morn, the nineteenth of May, recorded for ever the famous Ninety-two, brave Russel did discern, by break of day, the lofty sails of France advancing too. All hands aloft, they cry, let Bri-tish valour shine, let fly a culverine, the sig-nal of the line, let ev'ry man

MISCELLANY. 331

supply his gun. Follow me, you shall see, that the

battle it will soon be won, follow me, you shall see

that the battle it will soon be won.

Tourville on the main triumphant rowl'd,
  To meet the gallant Russel in combat on the deep;
He led a noble train of heroes bold,
  To sink the English Admiral at his feet.
Now every valiant mind to victory doth aspire,
The bloody fight's begun, the sea is all on fire;
    And mighty fate stood looking on,
      Whilst a flood all of blood,
    Fill'd the scuppers of the rising sun.

Sulphur, smoak, and fire, disturbing the air,
  With thunder and wonder affright the Gallic shore;
Their regulated bands stood trembling near,
  To see the lofty streamers now no more:
At six o'clock, the red, the smiling victors led,
To give a second blow, the fatal overthrow:
    Now death and horror equal reign,
      Now they cry, run and die,
    British colours ride the vanquish'd main.

See they fly, amaz'd, thro' rocks and sands,
  One danger they grasp at to shun the greater fate,
In vain they cry for aid to weeping lands,
  The nymphs and sea-gods mourn their lost estate,
For evermore adieu, thou dazzling rising sun,
From thy untimely end thy master's fate begun:
    Enough, thou mighty god of war:
      Now we sing, bless the King!
    Let us drink to every British Tar.

SONG CLXXV.

OLD SLY HODGE.

Curtis was old Hodge's wife, for virtue none was ever such, she led so pure so chaste a life, She led so pure so chaste a life, Hodge said it was virtue over much. For says sly old Hodge

says he,   For says old sly Hodge says he,

Great talkers do the least d'ye see, great talkers

do the least d'ye see.

Curtis swore if men were rude,
She'd pull their eyes out, tear their hair;
My dear says Hodge, you're wondrous good,
My dear says, &c.
However let us nothing swear,
For says sly old Hodge, &c.

One night she dream'd a drunken fool,
Be rude in spite of her, wou'd fain,
She makes no more than with joint stool,
She makes no more, &c.
Fell on her husband might and main,
Still says sly old Hodge, &c.

By that time she had broke his nose,
Hodge made a shift to wake his wife,
Oh! Hodge says she, judge by these blows,
Dear Hodge, &c.
I prize my virtue as my life,
But says sly old Hodge, &c.

I dream'd a rude man on me fell,
However I his project marr'd,
Dear wife, says Hodge, 'tis mighty well,
Dear wife says Hodge, &c.
But next time, don't hit quite so hard,
For says old sly Hodge, &c.

SONG CLXXVI.

MY DEAR JOCKEY.

Andante.

My laddie is gone far a-way o'er the plain,

While in sorrow behind I'm forc'd to re-

main, Tho' blue bells and violets the hedges adorn,

Tho' trees are in blossom, and sweet blows the

When lads, and their lasses, are on the green met;
They dance, and they sing; and they laugh, and they chat;
Contented and happy, with hearts full of glee:
I can't without envy, their merriment see

Those pastimes offend me; my shepherd's not there:
No pleasure I relish, that Jockey don't share.
It makes me to sigh; I from tears scarce refrain,
    I wish my dear Jockey,
    I wish my dear Jockey,
    I wish my dear Jockey return'd back again,

But hope shall sustain me; nor will I despair:
He promis'd he would in a fortnight be here.
On fond expectation my wishes I'll feast;
For love my dear Jockey to Jenny will haste.
Then, farewell, each care; and, adieu, each vain sigh:
Who'll then be so blest, or so happy, as I?
I'll sing on the meadows, and alter my strain,
    When Jockey returns,
    When Jockey returns,
    When Jockey returns to my arms back again.

SONG CLXXVII.

BANKS OF THE TWEED.

As on the banks of Tweed I lay reclin'd, beneath a ver-dant shade, I heard a found more sweet than pipe or flute, sure more enchanting was not Orpheus' lute; while list'ning and amaz'd, I turn'd my eyes, the more I heard, the greater my surprise. I rose and follow'd,

Neither linnet or nightingale sing half so sweet;
And the soft melting strain did kind echo repeat;
It so ravish'd my heart, and delighted my ear,
Swift as lightning I flew to the arms of my dear.

She, furpriz'd, and detected, fome moments did ftand;
Like the rofe was her cheek, and the lilly her hand,
Which fhe plac'd on her breaft, and faid, Jockey I fear
I have been too imprudent: pray, how came you here?

For to vifit my ewes, and to fee my lambs play,
By the banks of the Tweed, and the groves, I did ftray:
But, my Jenny, dear Jenny, how oft' have I figh'd,
And have vow'd endlefs love, if you'd be my bride?
To the altar of Hymen, my fair one, repair,
Where the knot of affection fhall tie the fond pair:
To the pipe's fprightly notes the gay dance we will lead,
And will blefs the dear grove, by the Banks of the Tweed.

SONG CLXXVIII.

DE'IL TAK' THE WAR.

De'il tak' the war, that hur-ri'd Wil-ly frae me,

who to love me juft had fworn, they made him

captain fure to un - - do me, wae is me, he'll

ne'er re-turn, a thoufand loons a-broad will

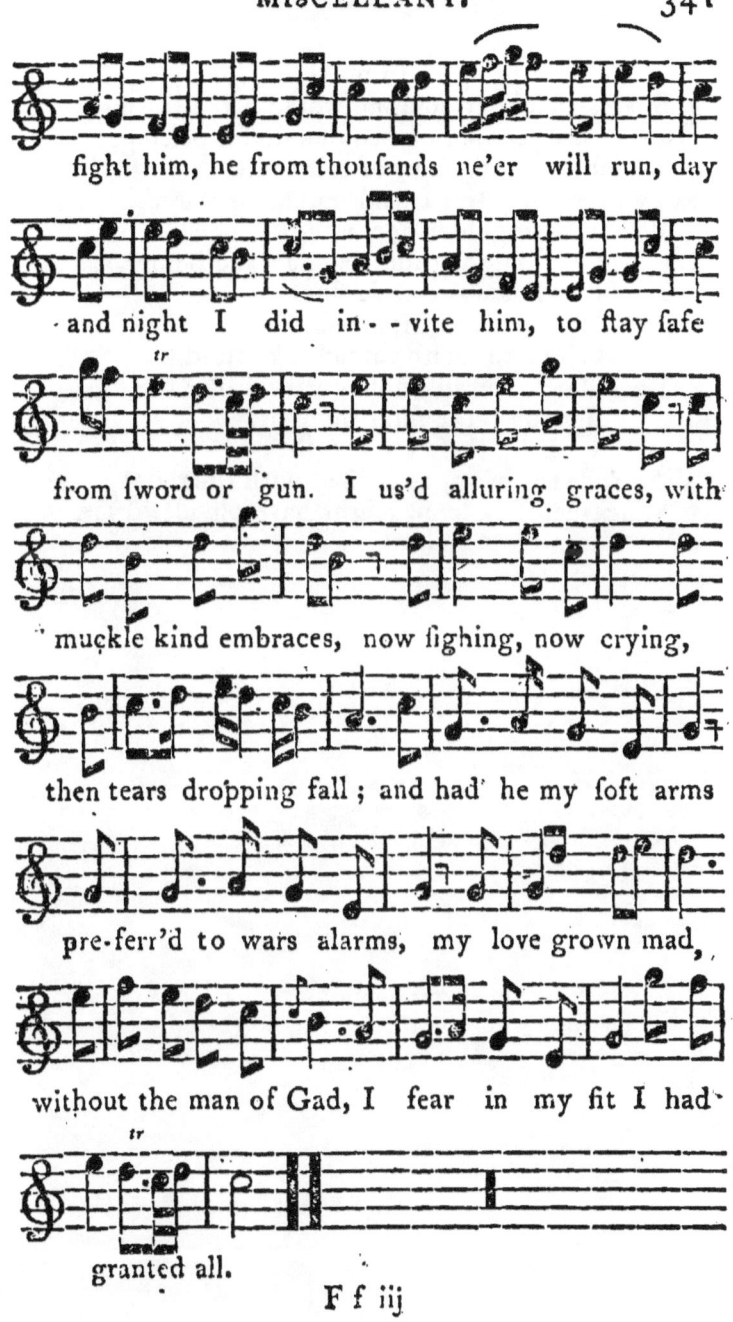

I wash'd, and patch'd, to make me look provoking;
  Snares that they told me would catch the men,
And on my head a huge commode sat poking,
  Which made me shew as tall again;
For a new gown too I paid muckle money,
  Which with golden flow'rs did shine;
My love well might think me gay and bonny,
  No Scots lass was e'er so fine.
    My petticoat I spotted,
    Fringe too with thread I knotted,
  Lace shoes, and silk hose garter'd o'er the knee;
    But, oh! the fatal thought,
    To Billy these are nought;
Who rode to towns, and rifled with dragoons,
  When he, silly loon, might have plunder'd me.

SONG CLXXIX.

Tune—*My sheep I've forsaken*—Page 292.

AH Chloe! thou treasure, thou joy of my breast,
Since I parted from thee, I'm a stranger to rest;
I fly to the grove, there to languish and mourn,
There sigh for my charmer, and long to return;
The fields all around are smiling and gay,
But they smile all in vain—my Chloe's away;
The field and the grove can afford me no ease,—
But bring me my Chloe, a desart will please.

No virgin I see that my bosom alarms,
I'm cold to the fairest, tho' glowing with charms,
In vain they attack me, and sparkle the eye;
These are not the looks of my Chloe, I cry.
These looks, where bright love, like the sun sits enthron'd,
And smiling diffuses his influence round;
'Twas thus I first view'd thee, my charmer amaz'd,
Thus gaz'd thee with wonder, and lov'd while I gaz'd.

Then, then the dear fair one was still in my sight,
It was pleasure all day, it was rapture all night;
But now by hard fortune remov'd from my fair,
In secret I languish, a prey to despair;
But absence and torment abate not my flame,
My Chloe's still charming, my passion the same;
O! would she preserve me a place in her breast,
Then absence would please me, for I would be bless'd.

SONG CLXXX.

JOVE IN HIS CHAIR.

Jove in his chair, of the sky lord mayor, with

his nods men and gods keep in awe; when he winks

heaven shrinks, when he speaks hell squeaks earth's

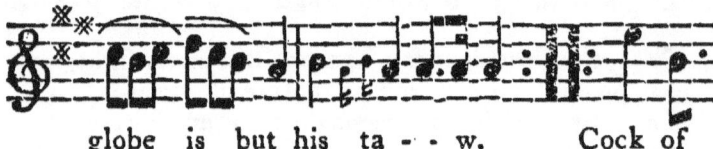
globe is but his ta - - w.   Cock of

the school, he bears despotic rule, his word tho'

absurd, must be law, even Fate, tho' so great, must

SONG CLXXXI.
GOOD NIGHT AND JOY BE WI' YOU.

How happy's he, who e'er he be, that in his lifetime meets one true friend, who cordially does sympathife in words, in ac-ti-on, heart, and mind. My kind, refpects do not ne-glect, although my wealth or ftate be fmall, with a melt-ing heart, and a mournful eye, I beg the Lord be with you all.

My loving friends, I kiss your hands,
   For time invites me for to move;
On your poor servant lay commands,
   Who is ambitious of your love.
He—whose pow'r and might, both day and night,
   Governs the depths, makes rain to fall,
To sun and moon gives course of light,
   Direct, protect, defend you all.

I do protest, within my breast,
   Your memory I'll not neglect;
On that record I'll lay arrest,
   Hell's fury shall not alter it.
All I desire of earthly bliss,
   Is to be freed from guilt or thrall;
I hope my God will grant me this:
   Good-night, and God be wi' you all.

FINIS.

www.ingramcontent.com/pod-product-compliance
Lightning Source LLC
Chambersburg PA
CBHW020236240426
43672CB00006B/546